Chuck and Blanche Johnson's Savor Cookbook®

# *Savor*
# *Washington*
# *Cookbook*

## *Washington's Finest Restaurants*
## *Their Recipes & Their Histories*

Wilderness Adventures Press, Inc.™
Belgrade, Montana

© 2007 Chuck and Blanche Johnson
Photographs contained herein © 2007 as noted

Maps, book design, and cover design © 2007 Wilderness Adventures Press, Inc.™

Published by Wilderness Adventures Press, Inc.™
45 Buckskin Road
Belgrade, MT  59714
1-866-400-2012
Web site: www.wildadvpress.com
E-mail: books@wildadvpress.com

First Edition 2007

Printed in Singapore

ISBN  9-781932-09805-1    (1-932098-05-4)

OTHER TITLES AVAILABLE IN THIS SERIES:

Savor Arizona
Savor Colorado Mountains and Western Slope
Savor Denver and the Front Range
Savor Greater Seattle
Savor Idaho
Savor Michigan
Savor Montana II
Savor Oregon
Savor Portland
Savor Wild Game

# TABLE OF CONTENTS

## — Spokane —

*Table of Contents*

*Campers at Mt. Rainier National Park. Visitors to the park could rent tents at Longmire Springs and other places. Photo taken in 1922.*

*Ready to use saw on opposite side—17 feet accross undercut—Cedar in Washington.*

# INTRODUCTION

The State of Washington, along with its neighboring states and southwestern Canada, is the center of a unique style of cooking. Over the years, this culinary style has come to be known as "Pacific Northwest" cuisine. The rich abundance of foods in the entire state has provided both professional chefs and home cooks with the basis for creative cuisine with a special emphasis on local products.

Coastal Washington, along with its bays and estuaries, provides a wealth of seafood that truly defines the Pacific Northwest style. Salmon, halibut, flounder, and tuna, along with oysters, crab, and shrimp fresh from the sea are prepared in countless ways. Delectable mushrooms are found in forests throughout the state and utilized in much of Pacific Northwest cuisine.

The wide range of climate and terrain throughout the state gives rise to agricultural areas producing most of the products needed for a well-balanced and tasty diet. The farms and ranches of central and eastern Washington provide the perfect setting for growing wheat, barley, and other grains, as well as prime grazing land for beef and dairy cattle. The succulent fruits of the Northwest grow in abundance throughout the state. Washington leads the nation in the production of a wide variety of apples, but also grows delicious cherries, peaches, apricots, pears, blueberries, plums, and pluots.

And, of course, there are the magnificent wines of Washington State. While wine grapes were planted in the state as early as the mid-19th century, commercial wine production came into its own in the latter half of the 20th century. Today, the state ranks second in production of premium wines.

While an earlier book in our *Savor Cookbook Series* presented some of the fine restaurants in Seattle, this book takes the reader on a trip through the rest of this splendid state. Travel with us from the spectacular windswept coastline, through the Cascade Mountain Range to the soft, gently rolling terrain of eastern Washington and see how some of Washington's best chefs have utilized the bounty of the state.

It is important to note that all of the featured restaurants were by invitation. None of the restaurants were charged for appearing in this book. We selected them based on the excellence and uniqueness of their food, as well as their ambience. Many have interesting histories. We also looked for places that feature comprehensive wine lists. We want to thank the owners, managers, chefs, and all the restaurant staff members who participated in getting this project to fruition.

The reader can use this book in several ways. As a travel guide, the reader can learn something about a restaurant's history, philosophy, and ambience, as well as the type of cuisine that it features. The map in the front gives the reader a perspective of the state and approximately where each restaurant is located.

Reading the recipes is a fun way to get a "taste" of each restaurant, and trying them out at home can be fun for the home chef as well as his or her guests.

Enjoy,
Blanche and Chuck Johnson

# SAVOR WASHINGTON COOKBOOK

# Restaurants Featured

# WASHINGTON FACTS

*Sheep herder leads a large flock of sheep across the roadway over the Grand Coulee Dam. The spillway is partially visible to the right.*

**Admission to Statehood:**
November 11, 1889 (42nd)
**Eighteenth largest state in the union**
71,303 square miles
360 miles east to west
240 miles north to south
**Elevations** - Sea level to 14,410 feet
**Counties** - 39
**Population (2000)** - 5,894,121
29 Indian Reservations
120 State Parks
2 State Forests
3 National Parks
7 National Forests
30 Wilderness Areas
**Nickname**:
The Evergreen State

**Primary Industries:**
Farming
Lumber
Tourism
Computer Software
Aircraft
**Capital** - Olympia
**Bird** - Willow Goldfinch
**Flower** - Coast Rhododendron
**Tree** - Western Hemlock
**Fish** - Steelhead Trout

*U&I Bar, North Bend, Washington*

# Stars

## at Semiahmoo Resort

| | |
|---|---|
| 9565 Semiahmoo Parkway | **Breakfast** |
| Blaine, WA 98230 | Monday – Friday 6:30am – 11:30am |
| 360-318-2000 | Weekends 6:30am – Noon |
| 800-770-7992 | **Dinner** |
| www.semiahmoo.com | Tuesday – Thursday 5:00pm – 9:00pm |
| | Friday – Saturday 5:00pm – 10:00pm |

# Stars at Semiahmoo Resort

### Brian Pitcher, Executive Chef

Just ten miles from the U.S. – Canada border, Semiahmoo Resort provides the visitor with a plethora of activities. Nestled on a crescent-shaped point of land between Semiahmoo Bay and Drayton harbor, the resort offers a 300-slip saltwater marina, a full-service, European-style spa with complete exercise facility and an indoor/outdoor pool, as well as access to two of *Golf Digest's* "Top 100" public play courses that are open to play year round. The 1,100 acres of the resort are a natural wildlife preserve, providing wildlife and bird watchers a rich variety of species to view. The preserve is listed as one of the Audubon Society's top bird-watching spots.

The resort takes its name from the Native American Indian Salish language term meaning "half-moon," a perfect description of the curving coastline of the bay. The Semiahmoo band lived in family groups on the land until the late 19th century, when European and American settlers established a salmon cannery on the site. The three-masted sailing ships brought Alaskan salmon to the cannery, which became the largest facility of its kind on the West Coast. During the mid-20th century, as more stringent fishing regulations were introduced, the cannery diminished its production and was purchased in 1980 by the locally owned Trillium Corporation, which began developing the resort. Some of the original structures have been integrated into the resort's plan, including the original water tower.

After strolling the grounds and enjoying the myriad activities, diners can enjoy a romantic and relaxing dinner at the resort's premier restaurant, Stars. On Friday and Saturday evenings, a pianist enhances the mood with the strains from the baby grand piano. The earth-toned colors of the dining room complement the lovely views from the windows facing the water. And, as the light fades in the evening sky, the twinkling lights of White Rock appear across the bay in Canada.

The American cuisine is enhanced by the flavors of the Northwest with such offerings as Grilled King Salmon served with locally harvested mushrooms, English peas, and onion confit, and Roasted Long Line Cod with roasted fennel-onion, tomatoes, and smoked ham hock. For those who enjoy the bounty of the land, New York Steak "Marchands De Vin" is served with locally harvested mushrooms and Point Reyes bleu cheese. Also offered on a recent menu was a classy take on pork and beans: a bone-in pork chop served with Andouille sausage, bacon, ham hock, and cannelloni beans.

The award-winning wine list specializes in the best of the vineyards of Washington and California. Featuring over 1,500 bottles the collection has earned the *Award of Excellence* from the *Wine Spectator*.

 Award of Excellence

# Butternut and Apple Soup

This is one of our signature specialties and guest favorites.

## Ingredients

2 large onions, diced

2 cloves garlic, smashed

3 Granny Smith apples, cored and quartered

4 butternut squash, cut in half and roasted with oil, salt and pepper until soft

1 gallon chicken stock

1 quart heavy cream

## Preparation

SWEAT onions and garlic until soft. Add apples and cook for 10 minutes. Add stock and roasted squash (you don't have to peel them) and simmer for 30 minutes. Add cream and simmer for another 5 minutes.

REMOVE one-half gallon of stock and purée the rest of the mixture using the stock to adjust the consistency. Season with salt and pepper to taste and strain mixture through a small-holed china cap.

### Serves 5

# ORANGE ANISE GRANITA

This flavorful granita recipe creates a delicious sauce, perfect for topping fresh oysters.

## Ingredients

6 cups orange juice
1 cup champagne vinegar
3 star anise cloves
1 cup shallots, minced

½ serrano chile, minced
1 tablespoon salt
½ teaspoon pepper

## Preparation

COMBINE orange juice, champagne vinegar, and cloves in a saucepan over heat and reduce by half. Strain and add the shallots, serrano chile, salt, and pepper. Mix and freeze for at least one day or until frozen.

SCRAPE with a fork and serve on top of oysters.

*Yield: about 2 pints*

# BRAISED LAMB SHANKS

This is a great winter dish that pairs nicely with a side of golden Yukon mashed potatoes.

## Ingredients

| | |
|---|---|
| 6 lamb shanks, seasoned | 2 quarts red wine |
| olive oil | 1 gallon chicken stock |
| 3 carrots, rough-cut | 1 gallon veal stock |
| 2 heads fennel, rough-cut | 1 tablespoon fennel seeds |
| 2 large onions, diced | 2 sprigs rosemary |
| ½ cup garlic cloves, smashed | ½ bunch thyme |
| 3 quarts orange juice | |

## Preparation

PREHEAT oven to 350 degrees. Place a small amount of olive oil in a large pan and sear lamb shanks. Remove excess oil, add carrots, fennel, garlic, and onions and cook until vegetables are slightly browned.

ADD orange juice and wine and reduce by half. Add herbs and the add stock to cover. Bring to a boil and then transfer to 350-degree oven.

COOK for 1½ to 2 hours, or until the meat begins to come away from the bone. Remove shanks from liquid, strain liquid and pour the strained liquid back over the shanks. Cool.

REHEAT before serving.

*Serves 6*

# THE WINE SPECTATOR AWARD

**M**any of the restaurants included in this cookbook have been recognized by *Wine Spectator*, the world's most popular wine magazine. It reviews more than 10,000 wines each year and covers travel, fine dining and the lifestyle of wine for novices and connoisseurs alike. Through its Restaurant Awards program, the magazine recognizes restaurants around the world that offer distinguished wine lists. Restaurants are responsible for submitting their own lists.

Awards are given in three tiers. In 2006, 3,772 restaurants earned wine list awards. To qualify, wine lists must provide vintages and appellations for all selections. The overall presentation and appearance of the list are also important. Once past these initial requirements, lists are then judged for one of three awards: the Award of Excellence, the Best of Award of Excellence, and the Grand Award.

- Award of Excellence—The basic Award of Excellence recognizes restaurants with lists that offer a well-chosen selection of quality producers, along with a thematic match to the menu in both price and style.
- Best of Award of Excellence—The second-tier Best of Award of Excellence was created to give special recognition to those restaurants that exceed the requirements of the basic category. These lists must display vintage depth, including vertical offerings of several top wines, as well as excellent breadth from major wine growing regions.
- Grand Award—The highest award, the Grand Award, is given to those restaurants that show an uncompromising, passionate devotion to quality. These lists show serious depth of mature vintages, outstanding breadth in their vertical offerings, excellent harmony with the menu, and superior organization and presentation. In 2006, only 77 restaurants held Wine Spectator Grand Awards.

 Award of Excellence        Best of Award of Excellence

 Grand Award

# McMillan's
# Dining Room
## at Roche Harbor

ROCHE HARBOR
*Established 1886*

248 Reuben Memorial Drive
P.O. Box 4001
Roche Harbor, WA 98250
360-378-5757
www.rocheharbor.com

Summer Hours:
Nightly 5:00pm – 10:00pm
Winter Hours:
Thursday – Monday 5:00pm –
10:00pm

# McMillan's Dining Room at Roche Harbor

## William Shaw, Executive Chef

History casts a charming spell over the seaside village of Roche Harbor. In1787, Spanish Captain Lopez de Haro and his crew became the first Europeans to sail among the San Juan Islands. In 1845, the Hudson's Bay Company built a log trading post at the head of Roche Harbor. As the 19th century unfolded, both American and Canadian citizens settled in the area, creating a dispute called the "Pig War" as to which country laid claim to the islands. After arbitration, the San Juan Islands were awarded to the United States in 1872.

During this time, valuable lime deposits were discovered along the ridge above Roche Harbor, and were developed in the late 19th century. In the mid-1880s Tacoma lawyer, John S. McMillan, negotiated to buy the lime deposit claims and the property, and formed the Tacoma and Roche Harbor Lime Company in 1886, Mr. McMillan built the 20-room Hotel de Haro around the original Hudson's Bay Post. The hotel hosted many wealthy and famous guests, including a visit by President Theodore Roosevelt on July 13, 1906. John McMillan also built housing for the company workers, as well as a lavish house on the edge of the harbor for himself.

In 1956, all 4,000 acres with twelve miles of coastline were sold to Reuben J. Tarte, a Seattle businessman. He and his family set about restoring the old hotel and warehouse, and turning the area into a resort. Their renovations included restoring the McMillan home and opening McMillan's Dining Room as part of the resort. Then, in 1988, the family sold Roche Harbor Resort to the current owners, partners Rich Komen and SaltChuk Resources, Inc. of Seattle, who have continued the tradition of preserving the historic core of the village.

Housed in the beautiful white clapboard house, the McMillan's Dining Room offers award-winning Pacific/Northwest cuisine and upscale service to its guests, who come by both land and sea—the 377-slip marina at the resort offering very comfortable births for nautical visitors. Executive Chef William Shaw has created a bounty of Northwest-inspired cuisine for the restaurant. As Chef Shaw says, "When we work with the menus, we create food that evokes flavors inherent in local products—seafood and lamb from the island, locally Northwest produce and herbs, and so on. We want our wine selections to represent that theme, as well." Come and enjoy a relaxing evening in an historic setting, with the sun setting over the picturesque Roche Harbor marina and bay.

 Award of Excellence

# DUNGENESS CRAB BISQUE

One of my favorites, and one of the most requested recipes by both Canadian and American guests, is our Dungeness Crab Bisque. This rich cream base soup with puréed peppers, fresh herbs, and sweet local Dungeness crab served with a hot loaf of sourdough bread makes for a perfect lunch while boating in the Northwest. -William Shaw, Executive Chef

## Ingredients

1 medium carrot, peeled and rough cut
1 celery stalk, rough cut in 1-inch pieces
1 medium red bell pepper, rough cut
1 medium green bell pepper, rough cut
1 yellow onion, rough cut
1 clove garlic, puréed
1 tablespoon fresh parsley, minced
½ tablespoon fresh chives, ⅛-inch cut
1 teaspoon fresh tarragon, coarsely chopped
3 tablespoons whole butter

⅓ cup all-purpose flour
1 ounce brandy
2 tablespoons Spanish paprika
¼ cup Old Bay Seasoning®
¼ teaspoon black pepper, ground
dash cayenne pepper
1 tablespoon crab base
12 ounces milk
18 ounces heavy cream
4 ounces fresh Dungeness crabmeat

## Preparation

PLACE vegetables into a food processor with the garlic and process to a fine mince. Transfer ingredients into a large heavy-gauge saucepot. Add parsley, chives, and tarragon and heat over medium heat until the vegetables are al dente in texture.

IN another heavy-gauge saucepot, melt butter over medium heat. Whisk in the flour, creating a roux. Let the roux cook for 4–5 minutes, stirring frequently to prevent scorching. Reserve roux for later use.

ADD brandy to the vegetable/herb mix and deglaze. Add paprika, Old Bay Seasoning,® black pepper, cayenne pepper, and crab base. Let the mixture cook for an additional 3–4 minutes. Whisk in the milk and heavy cream and, stirring frequently, heat the bisque to an internal temperature of 160 degrees.

ADD the reserved roux and let the bisque cook over low heat until an internal temperature of 180 degrees is achieved, approximately 30–40 minutes. Stir frequently to prevent scorching the bottom of the pot. Bisque should be thick in consistency. When desired consistency is achieved, add crabmeat and cook until crab is heated through.

*Serves 4–6*

# STUFFED SINGING PINK SCALLOPS

Local singing pink scallops are filled with our rich Dungeness crab, artichoke, and Parmesan cheese, and then oven roasted.

## Ingredients

4 ounces fresh Dungeness crabmeat, drained

4 ounces marinated artichoke hearts, chopped into ½-inch pieces

2 ounces Walla Walla onion, sliced into ⅛-inch julienne

1 cup mayonnaise

2 ounces Parmesan cheese, grated fine

1 tablespoon flat leaf parsley, chopped fine

12 singing pink scallops, with top shell removed

vegetable oil

salt and pepper to taste

## Preparation

PREHEAT oven to 350 degrees. Place crab, artichokes, onion, mayonnaise, Parmesan and parsley into a medium-sized bowl. Stir until all ingredients are well combined. This mixture can be made up to two days in advance and stored in the refrigerator.

PLACE scallops on the half shell on an oiled baking sheet, leaving approximately 2 inches between each scallop. Season each scallop with a pinch of salt and pepper. Using a small rubber spatula or spoon, spread crab mixture on top of each scallop, covering the entire shell. Place in 350-degree oven until crab mixture begins to brown and slightly rise.

*Serves 4*

*Battleship Salmon.*

# LOCAL SOCKEYE SALMON
## *with Roasted Mushroom Mayonnaise*

With emphasis on our local bounty, this recipe uses sockeye salmon that is covered with roasted Northwest mushrooms that are folded into a seasoned mayonnaise and then roasted to medium-rare.

## Ingredients

- 6 ounces shiitake mushrooms, stems removed, sliced to ⅜ inch
- 6 ounces crimini mushrooms, sliced to ⅜ inch
- 6 ounces chanterelle mushrooms, sliced to ½ inch
- ¼ cup olive oil
- ½ teaspoon sea salt
- ¼ teaspoon freshly ground black pepper
- ½ teaspoon fresh rosemary, chopped fine
- 1 cup mayonnaise
- 2 tablespoons fresh lemon juice
- 1 tablespoon soy sauce
- 2 tablespoons flat leaf parsley, chopped fine
- 6 6-ounce filets of fresh wild salmon, skin removed and block cut

## Preparation

PREHEAT oven to 350 degrees. Place sliced mushrooms into a medium-sized bowl and add olive oil, salt, pepper, and rosemary. Toss until mushrooms are thoroughly coated. Spread seasoned mushrooms evenly on a baking sheet. Place in oven and bake until mushrooms begin to brown. Turn mushrooms over and bake until slightly crisp on the edges of the mushrooms. Allow to cool.

IN A medium-sized bowl, combine mayonnaise, lemon juice, soy sauce, and parsley. Add cooled mushrooms and gently fold them into the mayonnaise mixture.

PLACE salmon filets on an oiled baking sheet, leaving approximately 2 inches between each filet. Season filets with a pinch of salt and pepper. Using a small rubber spatula or spoon, spread mayonnaise/mushroom mixture on top of seasoned salmon filet, leaving the edges of salmon partially uncovered.

PLACE in 350-degree oven until salmon has an internal temperature of 125 degrees. If you like your salmon well done, cook until an internal temperature of 135–145 degrees is achieved.

*Serves 6*

# CEDAR PLANK ROASTED KING SALMON

## Ingredients

2 4-ounce fresh king salmon sides, skin on and pin bones removed (size of salmon should be no greater than 1½ inches thick)

1½ teaspoons Fish Dry Rub Seasoning (recipe follows)

juice of ⅛ of a lemon
your choice of rough-cut vegetables
1 tablespoon butter, melted
2 lemon wedges, for garnish

## Preparation

PLACE salmon skin-side down on sheet pan. Sprinkle the Fish Dry Rub Seasoning over all sides, except the skin side. Press seasonings into the salmon flesh. Refrigerate salmon steaks, uncovered, for at least 2 hours before using.

PREHEAT oven to 425 degrees. Oil and preheat a cedar plank. Place salmon pieces, skin-side down, between 3 o'clock and 9 o'clock on the preheated plank. Drizzle lemon juice over the top of the salmon pieces. Place vegetables between 10 o'clock and 2 o'clock on the plank, beside the salmon.

PLACE cedar plank in oven and bake for approximately 10–12 minutes, or until an internal temperature of 130 degrees is achieved. Remove cedar plank from oven and liberally baste top of salmon and vegetables with melted butter. Garnish with lemon wedges and serve.

*Serves 2*

## For the Fish Dry Rub Seasoning

2 teaspoons lemon pepper
1 teaspoon granulated garlic
1 teaspoon dry whole tarragon
1 teaspoon dry whole basil

1 tablespoon paprika
1 tablespoon kosher salt
2 teaspoons brown sugar

PLACE all ingredients into a food processor and process until well blended. Transfer into a small airtight container and store at room temperature until use.

# MEATLOAF WITH ROASTED MUSHROOM SAUCE

This popular comfort food is served at Roche Harbor's Madrona Room.

## Ingredients

- 3 ounces butter
- 1½ ounces green onions, thinly sliced
- ½ pound onions, chopped to ¼-inch
- 4 ounces celery, chopped to ¼-inch
- 5 ounces red bell pepper, chopped to ¼-inch
- 1 tablespoon garlic, minced
- 1½ tablespoons Worcestershire sauce
- ½ cup brandy
- 3 bay leaves
- 1 tablespoon kosher salt
- 1½ teaspoons black pepper
- 1 teaspoon white pepper
- 1 teaspoon cumin
- 1 teaspoon nutmeg
- ¾ cup heavy cream
- ¾ cup ketchup
- 1¾ pounds Black Angus ground beef
- ½ pound ground veal
- ¾ pound sausage pork
- 3 eggs, beaten
- 1½ cups panko breadcrumbs, processed through food processor
  Roasted Mushroom Sauce (recipe follows)
  chopped parsley, for garnish

## Preparation

PREHEAT oven to 350 degrees. In a large sauté pan over medium heat, melt butter and add onions, celery, bell pepper, garlic, Worcestershire sauce, brandy, bay leaves, and all seasonings and spices. Sauté until vegetables are tender and the mixture starts sticking to the pan, about 20–30 minutes. While cooking, stir mixture occasionally and scrape the pan bottom well, to prevent burning. Stir in heavy cream and ketchup. Continue cooking for about 2 minutes. Remove from heat and allow mixture to cool to room temperature. Remove and discard bay leaves.

PLACE the ground meats in a large mixing bowl and add beaten eggs, the cooked vegetables, and the breadcrumbs. Mix by hand until thoroughly combined. Place mix in a 4-inch deep pan and shape into a loaf. Bake in a 350-degree oven for 35 minutes, and then raise the heat to 400 degrees. Continue cooking for another 35 minutes. When done, the top should be brown and firm to the touch, and the internal temperature should be 135 degrees.
Let set at room temperature for 10 minutes. Then, holding the top, drain the grease. Let set for 2 hours at room temperature in the pan to cool. After cooled, hold the top and drain any excess grease.

TO SERVE, place slices of meatloaf on plates and drizzle about 2½ ounces of Roasted Mushroom Sauce over each slice. Garnish with chopped parsley.

*Serves 8–10*

## For the Roasted Mushroom Sauce

| | |
|---|---|
| 1 teaspoon lemon zest, minced | olive oil |
| ½ teaspoon sea salt | 16 ounces veal stock |
| 1 teaspoon black pepper, freshly ground | 1 tablespoon butter |
| 2 teaspoons fresh thyme, coarsely chopped | ½ ounce (by weight) garlic, minced |
| 1½ teaspoons fresh sage, coarsely chopped into ¼ pieces | 1 tablespoon flour |
| 1 8-ounce portobello mushroom, ¼-inch slices | 1 fluid ounce brandy |

PREHEAT oven to 400 degrees. Combine spices, herbs, and mushroom slices with a little olive oil, tossing to coat well. Transfer to a sheet pan and roast in oven until mushrooms are dark and golden brown, about 15–20 minutes. Cool mushroom mixture and set aside.

PLACE veal stock in saucepan over medium heat and reduce by 50%. Melt butter in another saucepan over medium heat. Add garlic and sauté until tender, then add flour, stirring to make a roux. Add reduced veal stock to roux mixture and bring to a slow rolling boil, stirring constantly. Reduce heat to low and add roasted mushrooms and brandy. Hold sauce on low temperature until service.

# Duck Soup Inn

50 Duck Soup Lane
Friday Harbor, WA 98250
360-378-4878
www.ducksoupinn.com

Dinner 5:00pm – 10:00pm
Seasonal Dining:
check schedule on website or call

# Duck Soup Inn

## *Gretchen Allison, Chef/Owner*

Tucked into the woods on a five-acre property overlooking several picturesque ponds, Duck Soup Inn has been serving residents and visitors for over thirty years. The location where the restaurant now sits was once used by the horse-drawn wagons that were making the ten-mile trip across San Juan Island, from Roche Harbor in the north to Friday Harbor in the southeast section of the island. Horses could get shod and watered at this halfway point. The building was originally a carpenter's workshop and, in 1975, three women—two sisters and their cousin—converted it into a restaurant. The wooded interior has booths and a fieldstone fireplace. In 1989, Chef Gretchen Allison bought the restaurant and property.

Born and raised in Burlingame, California, Gretchen started cooking at the age of sixteen in a local restaurant. She graduated from the California Culinary Academy in San Francisco in 1981 and went on to cook in the Bay Area, Hawaii, Massachusetts, and the U.S. Virgin Islands before landing on San Juan Island.

The first thing she did after buying the Duck Soup Inn was to establish a kitchen garden, which is located next door, on her parents' property. Soon after, full crops of organically grown herbs and edible flowers were being enjoyed. An orchard of plums, pears, and apples was already planted, so in late summer and fall the customers were enjoying pies and chutneys from home grown fruit. The local farmers, such as Nootka Rose and Pelindaba Lavender Farm, heavily supplement the restaurant's produce needs. There is excellent shellfish being raised on the island by Westcott Bay Sea Farms, and the wild fish catch is plentiful and fresh. Duck Soup Inn serves it in a variety of ways: smoked, cured, and fresh. They also smoke and cure a variety of meats and cheeses.

Although the emphasis is on fresh Northwest cooking, Gretchen's wide-ranging experience and her thirst for more exotic cuisines has led her to incorporate international touches to her culinary achievements. The pantry of spices grows every year as she entertains her restaurant guests with novel tastes. The seasonal menus are kept to a manageable size to insure the best quality at every dinner. Along with presenting masterfully prepared foods, Duck Soup Inn offers a well-rounded menu of wines and beers, as well as spirits, many of which have been combined with homemade herb infusions and fresh juices.

# Applewood Smoked Oysters
*with Fresh Herbs de Provence Mignonette*

I use a Little Chief brand smoker, available at most hardware stores. At the restaurant we use the Westcott Bay oysters that are farmed about a mile up the road from us. -Gretchen Allison, Chef/Owner

## Ingredients

3 dozen medium-small oysters
2 teaspoons non-iodized salt in 2 quarts
cold water
4 cups applewood shavings
rock salt

½ cup Reggiano Parmigiano, grated
¼ cup butter
2 tablespoons chives, chopped
Herbes de Provence Mignonette
(recipe follows)

## Preparation

SHUCK the oysters and discard the top shells. Loosen each oyster from the bottom shell by running the shucker under the oyster, cutting through the attaching muscle. Rinse each oyster in the salted water and rinse the shell to remove any loose bits of shell.

PREHEAT smoker. Replace oysters in their bottom shells, smoother side facing up (it looks nicer) and place on racks in the smoker. Smoke for 1 hour. After smoking to this stage they can last a few days, covered in the fridge, before continuing to the next step.

PREHEAT the oven to 500 degrees. Place ½ inch of rock salt in a baking pan and nestle the oysters into the salt. Sprinkle a pinch of Parmesan on top of each oyster and dab with ¼ teaspoon butter. Bake for about 8 to 10 minutes until browned and cooked through. Sprinkle with the chives. Spoon ½ teaspoon of Herbes de Provence Mignonette on each and serve.

### Serves 6 as an appetizer

## For the Herbs de Provence Mignonette

1 teaspoon grated lemon zest
½ cup lemon juice
¼ cup sherry vinegar
2 tablespoons shallots, minced
1 tablespoon fresh thyme leaves
2 tablespoons fresh Italian parsley
leaves

2 tablespoons fresh basil leaves,
chopped
2 teaspoons fresh rubbed lavender
flowers
1 teaspoon fresh rosemary, chopped
½ teaspoon salt
½ teaspoon freshly ground black pepper

STIR together just before serving.

# TOMATO, ONION AND CHILI SOUP WITH HERB PESTO

## Ingredients

½ cup butter
4 large onions, chopped
2 cups white wine
1 carrot, peeled and sliced
5 fresh mushrooms
3 or 4 assorted large chilies, roasted and skinned
6 large ripe tomatoes

1 teaspoon Spanish smoked paprika
2 teaspoons fresh thyme
1 bay leaf
3 quarts chicken stock (as needed)
salt and pepper
1 cup cream
Herb Pesto (recipe follows)
Sour Cream Garnish (recipe follows)

## Preparation

MELT butter in a large non-reactive pot. Add onions and sauté quickly, stirring constantly until browned around the edges. Add wine and reduce the heat. Allow the wine to evaporate and continue to cook the onions slowly until well-browned. Add the carrot, mushrooms, chilies, tomatoes, paprika, thyme, bay leaves, and chicken stock. Simmer for at least an hour, until the veggies are soft. Add more stock if needed. Purée in a blender and strain. Season with salt and pepper. Add the cream. Re-heat to serve. Ladle into warm bowls. Dollop with a spoon of Herb Pesto and drizzle with Sour Cream Garnish.

*Serves 8–10*

## For the Herb Pesto

½ cup parsley leaves
½ cup cilantro leaves and stems
½ cup basil leaves
½ cup olive oil

1–2 tablespoons lemon juice (to taste)
1 clove garlic
½ cup lightly toasted nuts
salt

PURÉE all ingredients in a food processor. Leave slightly coarse. Adjust seasoning and keep chilled. The pesto will keep for a few days.

## For the Sour Cream Garnish

3 tablespoons sour cream
1 tablespoon cream or water

MIX well and reserve for service.

# Fresh Pea and Dungeness Crab Omelet
### with Chèvre, Tarragon and Pea Tendrils

## Ingredients

| | |
|---|---|
| 1 tablespoon fresh peas | 1 tablespoon good quality chèvre, |
| 1 teaspoon shallot, minced | broken up |
| 2½ teaspoons butter, divided | 2 eggs |
| 2 tablespoons fresh-picked crabmeat | pinch salt |
| 1 teaspoon fresh tarragon, chopped | 1 grinding of pepper |
| 1 good squeeze lemon juice | Dressed Pea Tendrils (recipe follows) |

## Preparation

WARM a plate for service. Sauté the peas and shallot in 1 teaspoon of the butter. When peas are tender remove from the pan into a dish. Add the crab, tarragon, lemon juice, and chèvre to the dish. Set next to the stove where you will be working.

PLACE the eggs, salt, and pepper in a bowl and whisk together gently. Heat an 8-inch, good quality nonstick sauté pan over medium heat. Add the remaining butter and swirl to coat. When the butter foam subsides pour in the eggs all at once and, using a flexible spatula, begin lifting up the sides to allow the raw egg from the top to run underneath. When the egg no longer runs freely, remove from the heat and cover for a few moments to finish cooking any pools of raw egg on top.

WORKING quickly, place the filling down the center. Fold one third of the omelet over the filling. Position the pan over the plate and continue to roll the omelet out of the pan, landing seam-side down on the plate. Drape the Dressed Pea Tendrils over the top and serve.

### Serves 1

## For the Dressed Pea Tendrils

| | |
|---|---|
| 1 handful of 2-inch pea tendrils | ½ teaspoon grapeseed oil (or other oil of |
| pinch salt | choice) |
| pinch grated lemon zest | light squeeze lemon juice |

TOSS together. Set next to stove, beside the filling.

# SEARED ALASKAN SEA SCALLOPS
## *with Avocado and Pumpkin Seed Orange Dressing*

## Ingredients

⅓  cup baby greens
1  ripe avocado
1  orange, sectioned
1  tablespoon canola or peanut oil
8  ounces large Alaskan sea scallops,
    cleaned and patted dry

kosher or sea salt
Pumpkin Seed Orange Dressing
  (recipe follows)

## Preparation

ON two plates, arrange the greens in a small pile in the center of each. Halve and peel the avocado. Slice and arrange around the lettuce along with the orange sections.

HEAT a cast iron skillet with the oil over high heat until smoking. Sprinkle the scallops with a dusting of salt and add the scallops one at a time to the pan, well spaced to allow evaporation of the juices as they cook. When browned on one side, turn over and brown the other. Arrange the scallops around the avocado, orange sections and the greens. Drizzle with a few teaspoons of the Pumpkin Seed Orange Dressing.

*Serves 2*

## For the Pumpkin Seed Orange Dressing

juice of 1 lemon
1  teaspoon finely grated orange zest
1  tablespoon toasted pumpkin seed oil
2  tablespoons canola oil

2  teaspoons chopped tarragon, basil or
    mint (or a mix)
salt and pepper to taste

WHISK the ingredients to combine, and adjust tartness to taste with more oil or lemon.

# Hot Fudge Sauce

## Ingredients

1 cup cream
1 cup sugar
9 ounces high quality semi-sweet chocolate such as Callebau, chopped
⅓ cup corn syrup (this inhibits crystal growth)

## Preparation

OVER a double boiler melt the sugar into the cream. Stir occasionally until all of the sugar crystals are melted. Remove from heat and add the chocolate and corn syrup. Allow to sit until the chocolate is melted, then whisk until smooth. Serve warm over ice cream.

*Yield: about 2¼ cups*

# MALPOORA WITH FRESH PEACHES AND PISTACHIOS

## Ingredients

½ cup whole-wheat flour
½ cup all-purpose flour
1¾ cups cream, divided
1 cup milk
2 tablespoons water
4 tablespoons sugar
¼ teaspoon salt
1 egg

1 teaspoon crushed cardamom
2 tablespoons melted butter
   oil for the pans
2–3 ripe peaches, peeled, pitted and sliced
few tablespoons honey
¼ cup pistachios, chopped and lightly
   toasted

## Preparation

PLACE the flours, ¾ cup of the cream, milk, water, sugar, salt, egg, cardamom and melted butter in an electric blender and process until thoroughly blended. Cover and allow to rest at room temperature for ½ hour or so.

WHEN ready to cook the crêpes, slowly heat an 8-inch cast iron or non-stick pan to just before the smoking point. Rub the pan with 1 teaspoon of oil, using a paper towel wadded into a ball. The first crêpe is usually sacrificial so don't get discouraged. Here goes. Holding on to the handle with your left hand (if you are right handed) pour about 2 ounces of batter in the pan while rolling the pan in a circular motion to spread the batter over the bottom of the pan. Place the pan back on the heat. When it looks brown around the edges loosen around the edges with a spatula and flip it over to lightly brown the other side. Remove by flipping the pan upside down over a plate. Return the pan to the heat, re-oil it and pour in the next 2 ounces of batter. Repeat until the batter is gone. You can use more than one pan at a time to speed the process.

TO PEEL peaches easily, plunge them into boiling water for about 10 seconds then into cold water to prevent further cooking. The skins will rub right off.

TO SERVE, fold the crêpes into quarters and arrange on a warm platter. Drizzle with honey, arrange a few slices of peach on top and sprinkle with pistachios. Pass the pitcher with the remaining 1 cup of cream.

*Serves 4–6*

# PIE CRUST

A few pointers for good crust: Start with well-chilled (not frozen) ingredients and keep them cold during the whole process. Too much water makes for a tough crust. Leave chunks of butter as large as a small pea in the mix. Acid tenderizes flour, so buttermilk powder or a squeeze of lemon in the ice water is helpful.

## Ingredients

5½ cups all-purpose flour
2 teaspoons kosher salt
1 tablespoon sugar
2 tablespoons buttermilk powder

1 cup cold shortening
1¼ cup cold butter, cut into ½-inch cubes
4–6 ounces ice water

## Preparation

PLACE dry ingredients in a large food processor and mix briefly. Spoon in cold shortening and cold butter chunks. Pulse in 1-second intervals until the largest lumps are down to the size of a pea. Put the mix into a large stainless bowl and refrigerate while preparing the ice water. Drizzle the ice water over the mix, starting with about 4 ounces, and then toss with your finger tips to incorporate the water. Break up large wet lumps to distribute the water evenly. Usually the dough will need more water to hold together but be careful not to add too much at a time, for even a little too much water will make the dough tough. When you think you almost have enough water added, see if you can form a ball in your hands that doesn't completely crumble. If it holds together reasonably well, stop there. If not, crumble the dough back into the bowl and continue adding dribbles of water until you reach the desired texture. Gather the dough into 4 even balls and form into disks about ⅓-inch thick. Wrap each in plastic wrap and refrigerate or freeze.

TO BAKE an empty shell, preheat oven to 375 degrees. Roll 1 disk out on a floured surface so that it fits in an 8- or 9-inch pie pan and trim to a ½-inch overlap. Roll the edge over and flute the rim to make a pretty edge. Line the crust with foil and put a couple of cups of dry beans in to hold the foil in place. Press the beans out to the corners so that the foil is snugly against the crust. Bake in a 375-degree oven for 15 minutes, or until the rim starts to brown. Remove the foil and beans. Put the crust back in for 5 or 10 minutes to finish browning on the bottom. This is when I frequently burn the crust by thinking it will take longer than it really does. Remove when golden brown and cool before filling. Cooling allows the crust to crisp completely before adding ingredients that might absorb into a hot crust.

### Yield: 4 piecrusts

# WILD BLACKBERRY PIE

## Ingredients

4 cups fresh wild blackberries
¾ cup sugar
3 tablespoons cornstarch
1 teaspoon lemon zest
1 tablespoon lemon juice

2 disks of uncooked piecrust (see recipe in this section)
2 tablespoons buttermilk or milk
1 tablespoon raw sugar for the top

## Preparation

PREHEAT the oven to 375 degrees. Toss together the blackberries, sugar, cornstarch, zest and lemon juice.

ROLL out 1 disk of crust to fit into a 9-inch pie plate (I like glass because you can see when the bottom has browned enough and the glass heats evenly). Fit the crust into the plate with at least a ¼-inch overhang. Mix the filling to redistribute the sugar and mound it into the crust. Roll out the top crust and fit it over the fruit. Turn the crust edge under and pinch together while fluting the rim with your thumb and forefingers. Make a few small slits in a decorative pattern on top. Brush the top with buttermilk or milk and sprinkle with raw sugar.

PLACE in 375-degree oven and bake, turning during baking to brown evenly. Bake for 45 minutes or an hour, until it looks bubbly. Remove to a rack to cool. Don't refrigerate. Serve with whipped cream, crème fraîche or ice cream.

# WILD HUCKLEBERRY PEAR PIE

I am a fan of clear fruit flavors so will rarely add spices like cinnamon or clove to a pie. We get a big box of wild huckleberries from a friend who picks them in the Olympic Mountains. In the fall he shows up at the kitchen door with them and I stock my freezer for the months to come. I prefer using Bosc pears in my pies.

## Ingredients

4 cups of ripe pears such as Bosc, peeled and thinly sliced — about ⅛-inch thick slices

1 cup fresh or frozen wild huckleberries

¾ cup sugar

2 tablespoons instant tapioca or 1 tablespoon cornstarch

1 teaspoon lemon zest

1 tablespoon lemon juice

2 disks of uncooked piecrust (see recipe in this section)

milk or cream for glazing

1 tablespoon raw sugar for the top

## Preparation

PREHEAT the oven to 375 degrees. Prepare the pears, place in a bowl with the huckleberries, sugar, tapioca, lemon zest and juice, and toss to combine.

ROLL out 1 disk of crust to fit into a 9-inch pie plate, (I like glass because you can see when the bottom has browned enough and the glass heats evenly.) Fit the crust into the plate with at least a ¼-inch overhang. Mix the filling to redistribute the sugar and mound it into the crust. Roll out the top crust and fit it over the fruit. Turn the crust edge under and pinch together while fluting the rim with your thumb and forefingers. Make a few small slits in a decorative pattern on top. Brush the top with milk or cream and sprinkle with raw sugar.

BAKE in 375-degree oven, turning to brown evenly. Bake for 45 minutes or an hour, until a knife can be slipped through the filling without too much resistance and it looks bubbly. Remove to a rack to cool. Don't refrigerate. Serve with whipped cream, crème fraîche or ice cream.

# LEMON VANILLA ICE CREAM

## Tips for making ice cream:

1. Use lots of egg yolks for a smooth texture.
2. Don't use all cream; the result is greasy on the tongue. Use about ½ cup milk to every cup of cream. The milk adds protein without the fat.
3. For fruit ice cream, use fruit purée instead of milk and add some powdered milk to get the protein in.
4. Too little sugar will allow the formation of large ice crystals. Too much sugar will inhibit freezing. If making ice cream without a recipe, shoot for the sweetness of commercial ice cream.

## Ingredients

| | |
|---|---|
| 6 egg yolks | 2 teaspoons vanilla paste, or 2 |
| 2 cups cream | teaspoons vanilla extract, or ½ vanilla |
| ¾ cup sugar | bean, seeds scraped into cream |
| 1 cup milk (or evaporated milk for a | 2 teaspoons finely grated lemon zest |
| richer taste) | pinch salt |

## Preparation

WHISK the yolks, cream, and sugar over a double boiler until thickened. Add remaining ingredients and cool. Freeze in ice cream maker.

NOTE: Lemon juice is left out of this recipe because it tends to curdle the cream.

### *Yield: about 1 quart*

*Dick & Carol*

# Il Posto
## Ristorante Italiano

*Thank you so much for all your support!*

*Roselle & Mike*

il posto
RISTORANTE ITALIANO

**2120 Commercial Avenue**
**Anacortes, WA 98221**
**360-293-7600**

**Dinner Wednesday through Monday**
**from 4:00pm**

# Il Posto Ristorante Italiano

### *Isabella Valerio, General Manager / Owner*
### *Marcello Guiffrida, Executive Chef / Owner*
### *Sean Gervais, Chef*

The beautiful seaside town of Anacortes sits at the northern tip of Fidalgo Island, just north of Whidbey Island. Although people have lived in the Fidalgo and Guemes Island areas for more than 10,000 years, the first white people established claims on Fidalgo Island in the 1850s. Over the decades, the settlers evolved from hunters and trappers to farmers, ranchers, and commercial fishermen.

Their descendents have created a friendly, close-knit community that is attracting many newcomers to the area. Anacortes is a natural haven for artists, who are encouraged and supported by the community. Out of this support has emerged the Anacortes Mural Project that has been a two-decade endeavor for local artist Bill Mitchell. The life-size murals decorate over 90 locations in the town and feature portraits of some of Anacortes founders and favorite characters, as well as historic and nostalgic scenes of days gone by.

This special atmosphere in Anacortes played a part in bringing two very close friends to the area to open an authentic Italian eatery that has become a part of this caring community. Isabella Valerio and Marcello Guiffrida, both natives of Italy, have been friends for over thirty years. They came to Anacortes from Michigan, where Marcello had managed several highly regarded Italian restaurants, including Il Posto Ristorante in Southfield and the award-winning Bacco in Farmington Hills, Michigan.

Isabella and Marcello opened their restaurant in Anacortes on June 22, 2005 and it has become a haven for all who love the robust flavors of Italian cooking. It features old country cooking that includes homemade pastas and breads, which are the result of the dedication of Isabella's mother. She spent three months at the restaurant training the staff in the delicate art of pasta making and bread baking. The menu items are printed in Italian, and mouthwatering descriptions of each dish follow. Guests will find dishes from almost every region of Italy on the menu. The wine list features a comprehensive selection of domestic wines, along with a full selection of Italian wines, each followed by a full description for those who are not familiar with the wines of Italy.

Isabella's and Marcello's long-standing friendship is based on a shared passion for good food and good wine, and this passion is shared with the guests of Il Posto Ristorante Italiano. To quote Isabella, "The Italian way of living is defined by a love of good food, a passionate devotion to flavor, and a vibrant lifestyle. Our goal is to share with friends and family eating for enjoyment, health, and good living. Every meal is an opportunity to gather together and celebrate life. Buon Appetito!"

# Insalata Vigna

## Ingredients

1 pound mixed greens
Raspberry Vinaigrette (recipe follows)
1 cup walnuts

1 cup dried cranberries
1 cup Gorgonzola cheese, crumbled

## Preparation

PLACE mixed greens in a bowl and toss with the Raspberry Vinaigrette. Divide salad onto salad plates and garnish with walnuts, cranberries and sprinkle with the Gorgonzola crumbs.

*Serves 8*

## For the Raspberry Vinaigrette

1 lemon, juice of
¼ cup raspberry vinegar
2 teaspoons honey
salt & pepper to taste

1 cup extra virgin olive oil
1 cup mixed berries, blended

IN A stainless steel bowl place squeezed lemon juice, vinegar, honey, and salt & pepper. Whisk the preparation until it is uniform. While whisking, slowly add the extra virgin olive oil. Once olive oil is added, add the mixed berry sauce into the dressing and continue to whisk until oil and vinegar are mixed together.

# CARPACCIO DI MELANZANE

## Ingredients

3 eggplants, thinly sliced
  salt and pepper to taste
2 cups extra virgin olive oil
3 red onions, cut into thin rings
1 cup hot water
½ cup red wine vinegar

2 tablespoons sugar
1 pound goat cheese
½ cup roasted pine nuts
1 cup parsley, finely chopped
  Balsamic Reduction (recipe follows)

## Preparation

PREHEAT a grill to medium heat. Sprinkle salt and pepper and lightly brush the eggplant slices with some of the olive oil. Place the eggplants on a grill, flipping the slices to create grill marks for presentation. Once cooked, move slices off the fire and place on a plate. Place plate aside.

IN A sauté pan, braise the onions with olive oil until lightly golden. Combine the hot water and red wine vinegar and add the sugar, stirring until sugar is dissolved. Add this solution to the pan with the onions and allow it to simmer until all the liquid has evaporated.

TO SERVE, lay the grilled eggplant onto serving plate. Top with caramelized onions, goat cheese, pine nuts, and parsley. Garnish with Balsamic Reduction.

*Serves 8*

*Wine Suggestion: Prosecco Bisol "Jeio"*

## For the Balsamic Reduction

2 cups aged balsamic vinegar
1 tablespoon sugar

PLACE balsamic vinegar and sugar in saucepan at medium heat. Reduce contents of saucepan to ½ cup of ingredients and take it off the heat. Let cool off at room temperature. Once cooled, place reduced sauce into dressing bottle.

# STROZZAPRETI NORCINA

## Ingredients

¼  cup extra virgin olive oil
3  pounds sausage
1  onion, minced
8  cloves garlic, minced
2  cups white wine
3  pounds fresh tomato sauce
2  cups heavy cream

white truffle oil to taste
3  pounds strozzapreti pasta
   (squiggly-shaped rustic pasta)
1  cup parsley, finely chopped
   Parmigiano to taste
   salt and pepper to taste

## Preparation

IN A saucepan on high heat, heat extra virgin olive oil and add sausage, onion, and garlic and sauté for a few minutes until onions are golden. Add white wine and let the mixture simmer until wine is evaporated; then add the tomato sauce. Bring it to a boil and reduce heat and allow sauce to simmer. After 10 minutes add heavy cream and truffle oil, stir and continue to simmer for an additional 10 minutes.

WHILE the sauce is simmering, in a separate pot bring water to boil with salt and add the pasta and cook to desired texture. Once pasta is cooked, strain pasta well.

ADD pasta to saucepan and toss it until pasta is well mixed with sauce. Add the parsley and the Parmigiano to taste, and continue to toss pasta for a few more minutes to allow pasta to absorb the flavor of the sauce. Serve on plate and top with freshly grated Parmigiano.

### *Serves 8*

*Wine Suggestion: Rubino "La Palazzola"—Mostly Cabernet with some Sangiovese and some Merlot. Nose is full with rich, ripe red berry fruitiness, leather and sweet tobacco.*

# PANNA COTTA

## Ingredients

|   |   |
|---|---|
| 4 | gelatin (cola de pesce) sheets |
| ¼ | gallon heavy cream |
| ½ | cup half-and-half |
| 1 | cup sugar |
| few drops | vanilla extract |

2 ounces Grand Marnier
1 cup blended berries sauce
whipped cream and fresh mint leaves,
for garnish

## Preparation

DIP gelatin into a bowl of water at room temperature and allow gelatin to soften for 15 minutes. Place heavy cream, half-and-half, sugar, and vanilla extract into saucepan and bring to boil on low heat, while constantly stirring. When contents begin to boil, take away from flame, add Grand Marnier and stir.

SQUEEZE extra water from gelatin sheets and place gelatin into saucepan while continuing to stir for a couple more minutes. Transfer contents of the saucepan into a pouring container while straining any large pieces of gelatin remaining in the mixture.

POUR contents into smaller containers (cup or glasses or disposable aluminum containers) and place in refrigerator for 8 hours. When mixture becomes firm, the custard is ready.

TO SERVE, pour some of the berry sauce on each serving and garnish with whipped cream and a few leaves of fresh mint.

*Serves 8*

# Christopher's
## on Whidby

105 NW Coveland Street
Coupeville, WA 98239
360-678-5480
www.christophersonwhidbey.com

Lunch Monday through Friday
11:30am – 2:00pm
Saturday and Sunday
12:00pm – 2:30pm
Dinner Nightly starting at 5:00pm

# Christopher's on Whidbey

### *Andreas Wurzrainer, Chef/Owner*
### *Christy Reid, Sous Chef*

In January 2002, Andreas Wurzrainer purchased Christopher's Front Street Café in order to pursue his culinary dreams and create a more relaxed lifestyle for himself and his wife, Lisa, and children, Sebastian and Tia. The restaurant had been a fixture in Mariner's Court on Front Street for quite a few years, and Andreas continued the tradition for another four and a half years at that location. In May 2006, however, he moved the restaurant a block away to a newly constructed building on the corner of Coveland and Alexander Streets, and the name was changed to Christopher's on Whidbey. The new location offers guests a more contemporary space with windows on three sides and ample parking. Wide window frames painted a crisp white accent the rust and sienna colored walls, and the contemporary light fixtures softly illuminate the graining in the light wood tabletops. Corynn Youderian, who has been with the restaurant since January 2002, graciously and efficiently handles the front of the house, making each guest feel welcome.

Chef Andreas served a traditional, three-year cooking apprenticeship in his homeland of Austria. After several years as a Sous Chef in Munich, Germany, he achieved his Master Chef certification graduating with honors. This led to a nineteen-year career in the culinary arts serving first in chic European restaurants and then aboard luxury cruise liners that plied the waters of both the northern and southern hemispheres. It was on board one of these ships that Andreas met his wife-to-be, Lisa, who called Seattle home. Not long after their marriage, they decided to abandon the seafaring life for a home in Seattle, in order to begin a family. Andreas soon was offered a position at the Olympic Four Seasons Hotel, and was also involved in the grand opening of the Cascadia Restaurant in the Belltown area of Seattle. However, the highly competitive and trendy culinary atmosphere in fast-paced Seattle soon had the couple longing for a more serene atmosphere in which to raise their children. On a visit to Lisa's parents home in Greenbank, the family decided to make Whidbey Island their home.

Although Chef Andreas successfully executed the upscale culinary scene, he knew that he really wanted to prepare the kind of wholesome, down-to-earth kind of food he liked to serve friends and family in his own home. At Christopher's on Whidbey he has managed to make this dream a reality. He says that every meal he prepares must meet his five criteria: It must be delicious, ample, affordable, and the ingredients must be of high quality and as fresh as possible. From the reactions of the satisfied diners, he has obviously achieved his goal.

# CHRISTOPHER'S ON WHIDBEY CORN SALMON CHOWDER

This chowder is wonderful on a cool Whidbey Island summer evening, served with a basket of our crusty La Brea bread and a refreshing glass of rosé.

## Ingredients

2 ounces bacon, diced
1 medium onion, chopped
2 ounces white wine
1 cup heavy cream
1 cup vegetable stock
1 large russet potato, peeled and cubed

1 cup fresh corn kernels
2 medium tomatoes, seeded and diced
  salt & black pepper to taste
6 ounces salmon, diced
  fresh basil, for garnish

## Preparation

IN A medium-size soup pot, render bacon until almost crisp. Drain off half of the fat. Add onions and sauté until soft. Deglaze with wine. Add cream and vegetable stock. Bring to a simmer. Add cubed potatoes and let simmer until potatoes are fork tender. Add corn, diced tomatoes, salt, pepper, and diced salmon. Let simmer for about 5 minutes, stirring frequently. Re-season to taste. Top with fresh basil.

*Serves 4–6*

*Wine Suggestion: Barnard Griffin Rosé of Sangiovese, Washington*

# GRILLED HALIBUT
*served over Penn Cove Mussels and Vegetables in a Smoked Paprika Broth*

Halibut is one of our best selling dishes in the summer, when the fish is coming directly from Alaska or the waters off the coast of Washington State. This recipe we have found to be particularly popular.

## Ingredients

4 *6-ounce halibut fillets*
*canola oil*
1 *pound Penn Cove mussels, cleaned and bearded*
1 *medium yellow onion, sliced*
1 *red bell pepper, deseeded and sliced*
1 *tablespoon smoked paprika*
1 *cup white wine*

2 *medium tomatoes, deseeded and cut in strips*
1 *zucchini, sliced*
1 *bunch spinach, de-stemmed and washed*
½ *cup butter*
*lemon thyme, chopped*
*salt and pepper to taste*

## Preparation

PREHEAT barbecue grill. Season halibut fillets with salt and pepper. Spray halibut with a canola oil spray. Grill on barbecue for approximately 4 minutes on each side. Put aside. Sauté mussels, onion, and red pepper in canola oil just until mussels begin to open. Add smoked paprika and let roast for 1 minute. Add white wine, tomatoes, zucchini, and spinach. Let simmer until mussels are fully open. Stir in butter until melted. Add lemon thyme, and salt and pepper if needed.

PLACE mussels in a bowl and top with grilled halibut and fresh lemon thyme. Enjoy!

*Serves 4*

*Wine Suggestion: Snoqualmie Vineyard, Naked Riesling*

# Bacon Wrapped Pork Tenderloin with Mushrooms

A classic on our menu, it has been one of our most popular dishes from the day we opened. We serve this dish with a smoked cheddar cheese potato au gratin and steamed broccoli.

## Ingredients

| | | | |
|---|---|---|---|
| 2 | pork tenderloins (12–16 ounces each) | 14 | mushrooms, sliced |
| | fresh oregano, chopped | 3 | shallots, minced |
| | salt & black pepper | 3 | garlic cloves, minced |
| 14 | bacon slices | 4 | ounces white wine |
| | canola oil | 2 | ounces butter |

## Preparation

PREHEAT oven to 400 degrees. Cut tenderloins into 2-ounce pieces and season lightly with salt, fresh ground pepper, and fresh oregano. Wrap each piece with a slice of bacon. Heat sauté pan over medium heat. Add canola oil and sear tenderloins on both sides until golden brown. Put tenderloins on baking sheet and place in 400-degree oven for about 8 minutes.

IN the same pan, sauté mushrooms, shallots, and garlic until mushrooms are browned. De-glaze pan with wine. Season with salt, pepper and more fresh chopped oregano to taste. Add butter and stir until melted.

TO SERVE, place tenderloins on plates and top with mushrooms.

### Serves 4

*Wine Suggestion: Sonnhof Grüner Veltliner, Austria*

# APPLE CRÊPES

We change our crêpe fillings with the seasons. In the spring and summer, we use fresh Whidbey Island strawberries and raspberries, followed by peaches, and then apples in the autumn and winter.

## Ingredients

1 tablespoon butter
2 tablespoons brown sugar
2 Gala apples, peeled, cored and sliced
1 Granny Smith apple, peeled, cored and sliced
4 ounces apple juice

cinnamon, to taste
Crêpes (recipe follows)
vanilla ice cream
walnuts, for garnish
powdered sugar, for garnish
diced apple slices, for garnish

## Preparation

HEAT frying pan, add butter, brown sugar, and apples and sauté for about 5 minutes. Add apple juice and cinnamon and simmer for 5 minutes more.

FILL crêpes with hot apple filling. Top with vanilla ice cream and walnut halves. Garnish with powdered sugar and dried apples.

*Serves 4–6*

## For the Crêpes

2 eggs
1 cup heavy cream
2 ounces flour, sifted

salt
sugar

BLEND eggs and heavy cream together. Mix in flour gradually until it is a smooth consistency. Add salt and sugar to taste. Heat a 6-inch non-stick pan to medium heat. Spray pan with non-stick spray. Pour in enough batter to cover bottom of pan with a thin layer. Cook until light brown on the bottom. Flip with spatula. Cook for another 10–20 seconds until lightly browned.

# The Inn at Langley

THE INN AT
LANGLEY

400 First Street
Langley, WA 98260
360-221-3033
www.innatlangley.com

Dinner Friday and Saturday at 7:00pm
Dinner Sunday at 6:00pm
Dinner Thursday at 7:00pm
(summers only)
Pre fixe menu – reservations required

# Chef's Kitchen Restaurant at The Inn at Langley

## Matt Costello, Chef/General Manager

Built on a bluff overlooking the Saratoga Passage and the Cascade Mountains, the Inn at Langley is just a short distance from Seattle, Washington. A short drive and a ferry ride will bring you to the seaside village of Langley with its art galleries and antique shops. The inn offers a unique setting with its 26 guest rooms and cottages. Each accommodation has a 180-degree waterfront view from floor-to-ceiling windows, and a whirl bath jetted tub facing both the fireplace and the sea. From private decks, guests can watch the sun rise above the Cascade Mountains on the mainland or set over the Saratoga Passage.

Guests can be luxuriously pampered at the Spa Essencia, located at the beach level of the inn.

Chef Matt Costello and his team have created a special type of culinary pampering at the Chef's Kitchen Restaurant. Every Friday, Saturday, and Sunday, Chef Costello prepares an elaborate pre fixe six-course dinner for the inn's guests as well as for visitors. Wines from the extensive wine list, including many half-bottle selections, can also be purchased, or guests can choose a wine pairing specially selected for the evening's menu.

Chef Costello started in the restaurant business in 1989 at the Four Seasons Olympic Hotel in Seattle. In 1994, he joined famous Seattle Chef Tom Douglas. He headed up the kitchen at both Dahlia Lounge and Palace Kitchen. While chef of Palace Kitchen in 1996, the restaurant was nominated for the James Beard Award for the *Best New Restaurant* in the nation. And in 1998, *Seattle Magazine* named him *Best Chef in Seattle*. Under Costello's' direction, Dahlia Lounge was named *Seattle Weekly's 2001 Best Restaurant in the City*.

At the Chef's Kitchen Restaurant, Chef Costello is continuing his culinary artistry. His dedication to creating delicious repasts is anchored in a philosophy of using seasonal ingredients that can be obtained locally, whenever possible. This is made easier with the lovely formal herb garden located in the inn's own gardens. In addition, much of the produce is purchased from Whidbey Island gardeners.

The dining room is at the heart of the inn, overlooking the herb garden. Intimate tables are set up by the double-sided river rock fireplace and near the floor-to ceiling windows. A communal table that seats ten is positioned directly in front of the open display kitchen, allowing the guests a peak at the culinary action.

# BROWN BUTTER SCALLOPS
*with Caramelized Apricots and Arugula*

## Ingredients

1 cup cream
1 cup butter
2 ounces lemon juice
8 large sea scallops
   salt & pepper to taste
   olive oil

Caramelized Apricots (recipe follows)
tiny arugula leaves dressed with olive
oil & lemon, for garnish
toasted & crushed apricot kernels, for
garnish (optional)

## Preparation

IN A heavy-bottomed saucepan, cook the cream and butter until it separates and resembles grains of sand and is toasty brown. When the sauce is light brown, add lemon juice and continue to cook until the sand texture is achieved. Remove from heat and set aside.

SEASON scallops with salt and pepper and sear in olive oil in a sauté pan until rich brown. Flip scallops over and continue cooking for 2 minutes.

TO SERVE, arrange the Caramelized Apricots on a warm plate and place the scallops on top. Spoon the browned butter sauce around the sides. Garnish the plate with a few leaves of dressed arugula and the toasted apricot kernels.

*Serves 2*

## For the Caramelized Apricots

4 nearly ripe apricots (sugar present)
2 tablespoons butter

2 tablespoons sugar
½ lemon

PREHEAT oven to 300 degrees. Halve and pit the apricots, reserving the pits for use in the garnish if desired. Place a large sauté pan on medium-high heat and add the butter. Place the apricots in the pan, cut side down, and sauté until they begin to color. Sprinkle sugar on and swirl to caramelize. When the color is amber, toss the apricots in the caramel to coat, then squeeze lemon juice over all. Keep warm in oven until service.

# KING SALMON

## with Split Peas, Penn Cove Mussels, and Spinach

## Ingredients

- 4 ounces thick-cut bacon strips, cut into ½-inch pieces
- 3 cups chicken stock (or a mix of stock and water)
- 1 cup dry split peas
- 6 ounces Penn Cove mussels, scrubbed and debearded
- 2 shallots, thinly sliced, divided
- ¾ cup dry white wine
- 7 tablespoons unsalted butter, divided
- ⅓ cup lovage or flat-leaf parsley, chopped (plus extra for garnish)
- ¼ cup freshly squeezed lemon juice, divided
- 1 tablespoon olive oil
- 4 6-ounce wild salmon fillets, skin and pin bones removed
- salt & white pepper to taste
- ¾ pound spinach, rinsed, dried, and tough stems removed

## Preparation

PREHEAT oven to 375 degrees. In a medium skillet over medium-high heat, cook bacon until browned and crisp, about 5–7 minutes. Spoon bacon onto paper towels to drain and set aside.

PUT chicken stock in a medium saucepan and add split peas. Bring just to a boil over medium-high heat, then reduce heat to medium and simmer until peas are nearly tender but not mushy—about 18 minutes. The liquid should not boil; reduce to medium-low if needed. Drain peas well and set aside in a bowl. Reserve the saucepan to reheat peas later.

COMBINE mussels, bacon, and half the shallots in a large saucepan. Add wine, cover pan, and set it over medium-high heat. Gently shaking pan occasionally, cook until the mussels are open, about 3–5 minutes. Remove pan from heat and discard any mussels that have not opened. Cut 4 tablespoons of the butter into pieces and add to the pan. Then add the lovage and half of the lemon juice and shake the pan to gently combine. Cover the pan and keep warm.

HEAT the olive oil in a large, ovenproof skillet, preferably non-stick, over medium-high heat. Season salmon fillets with salt and white pepper and sear fillets on one side until lightly browned, 1–2 minutes. Turn salmon over, transfer the skillet to the 375-degree oven and roast until just a touch of translucence remains in the center, about 6 minutes.

WHILE the salmon is cooking, melt 2 tablespoons of the butter in the reserved saucepan over medium heat, add split peas, and drizzle with 1 tablespoon of the lemon juice. Heat gently, stirring occasionally, just until the split peas are warmed through.

MELT the remaining tablespoon of butter in a large saucepan over medium heat. Add the remaining shallot and sauté until tender, 2–3 minutes. Add spinach, the remaining 1 tablespoon of lemon juice, and salt and pepper to taste. Cook, stirring occasionally, until the spinach is full wilted, about 1–2 minutes.

TO SERVE, spoon the warm split peas into large shallow bowls that have been warmed, and top each with a salmon fillet. Top the salmon with the spinach, and arrange the mussels around the salmon. Pour the broth around, scatter chopped lovage over all, and serve right away.

*Serves 4*

# CLOVE-SCENTED DUCK BREAST
## *on a "Panisse" with Balsamic Gastrique*

## Ingredients

4 Muscovy duck breasts, boneless
salt & pepper
1 teaspoon ground clove
Matt's "Panisse" (recipe follows)

balsamic gastrique
fresh dandelion or radish sprouts, for
garnish

## Preparation

PREHEAT oven to 350 degrees. Rub duck with salt, pepper, and clove. In a dry pan, sear the breasts over medium heat until the skin is crisp and fully rendered. This could take up to 20 minutes. Flip breasts and let bake an additional 2–3 minutes, then leave it to rest 4–5 minutes.

TO SERVE, place the warm "Panisse" on each plate. Slice duck breasts thinly, fanning over the "Panisse" and drizzle balsamic gastrique around. Grind fresh pepper around plate prior to serving. Fresh dandelion or radish sprouts add great freshness and color.

*Serves 4*

## For Matt's "Panisse"

1 cup half and half
1 medium orange
¼ teaspoon cayenne pepper
¼ cup chickpea flour

salt & pepper
all-purpose flour, for dusting
olive oil

BRING half and half to a simmer. Grate the zest of the orange directly over the pot of half and half, and then add cayenne pepper. Sift chickpea flour into a bowl and add it to the milk mixture, stirring like polenta. When thick, season with salt and pepper and pour mixture onto a sheet pan lined with plastic wrap. Have enough extra plastic wrap to pull over the top of the panisse and refrigerate for at least 4 hours, but not overnight. When mixture is set, cut with a 2-inch ring cutter and dust in all-purpose flour. Sauté in a heavy-bottomed pan with a little olive oil until golden brown on both sides.

# The Fireside
# Restaurant
## at Port Ludlow Resort

1 Heron Road     Dinner nightly starting at 5:00pm
Port Ludlow, WA 98365
360–437–7000
www.portludlowresort.com

# The Fireside Restaurant at Port Ludlow Resort

### Deneb Williams, Executive Chef
### Kevin Earl, General Manager

The Resort at Port Ludlow is just short drive from historic Port Townsend and a scenic ferry ride from Seattle. The resort offers breathtaking views of the Olympic Mountains beyond Ludlow Bay, and is ideal for romantic getaways as well as executive retreats and meetings. It offers 27 holes of world-class golf, a 300-slip marina, and spa services. It is at the heart of Port Ludlow's "Master Planned Resort," set up for residents investing in a different lifestyle with resort amenities at their disposal. Condominium-style accommodations are available, as well as the luxuriously appointed rooms in the Inn at Port Ludlow. Inspired by New England's classic coastal summer homes, the veranda-wrapped inn features rose and herb gardens and guest rooms with classic mission-style furnishings. All rooms have private balconies, fireplaces, and oversized whirl bath jetted tubs that look out to spectacular water views.

The Fireside Restaurant occupies a special place on the first floor of the inn, offering a warm, casual atmosphere in which to enjoy fine dining without pretense. The dining room is actually divided into several rooms, creating a more intimate atmosphere. The large windows let in the western light which highlights the crisp linen cloths on the well-appointed tables, and the richness of the spacious dark wood chairs. The outdoor veranda offers breathtaking views of the Olympic Mountains and the scenic marina for diners enjoying the warm summer days.

Executive Chef Deneb Williams has created a culinary showcase of his talents in managing the restaurant. At the age of twelve, he began his culinary training in the San Juan Islands. At the age of eighteen, he spent the next three years training under Chef Nancy Flume at The Adriatica in Seattle during the 1980s. After that, he immersed himself in craft brewing and winemaking, spending the next two years at Liberty Malt Supply and the Pike Place Brewing Company. This led him to Denver, Colorado and the venerable Wynkoop Brewing Company. After several positions in and around Denver, he joined the Cliff House at Pikes Peak. During his tenure, the restaurant won many top awards. But, after two decades of following his dream, Chef Williams returned home to the Pacific Northwest and the kitchens of the Resort at Port Ludlow. Here he has created a philosophy for the restaurant that is true to the bounty of the Pacific Northwest and its many local culinary treasures.

# Dungeness Crab and Potato Bisque

## Ingredients

4 large Dungeness crabs
½ pound butter
2 cups onions, chopped
2 cups leeks, chopped (tops reserved for Crab Stock)
½ cup shallots, chopped
½ pound flour

Crab Stock (recipe follows)
1 32-ounce can diced tomatoes
2 pounds potatoes, peeled & diced
1 cup heavy cream
1 tablespoon sherry vinegar
fried prosciutto, for garnish

## Preparation

CLEAN Dungeness crabs and squeeze liquid out of crabmeat. Use shells and liquid when preparing Crab Stock.

SAUTÉ onion, leeks, and shallots in butter until translucent. Do not brown. Add flour and toast on low heat for 3 minutes. Add Crab Stock and incorporate while stirring briskly. Bring mixture to a hard simmer, stirring constantly. Add tomatoes and potatoes and cook on medium-low heat for about 1½ hours, or until potatoes are tender. Using a hand blender, purée soup and strain through a fine mesh chinois.

TO SERVE, finish soup with the heavy cream and sherry vinegar. Ladle into bowls and garnish with the crabmeat and fried prosciutto.

### Yield: 4 quarts

*Wine Suggestion: A full-bodied California Chardonnay with buttery-oaky flavors would stand up to the bisque quite well.*

## For the Crab Stock

4 Dungeness crab shells & liquid from crabmeat
2 gallons water
30 ounces clam juice

1 tablespoon Old Bay Seasoning®
leek tops
thyme
parsley

COMBINE all ingredients in stockpot and simmer on medium-high heat until reduced by one-third.

# NOUVEAUX LOUIS

## Ingredients

½  cup Dungeness crabmeat
10–15  size 31–40 shrimp, cooked
½  cup lobster meat
½  cup cantaloupe melon balls
½  cup watermelon balls

2  ounces prosciutto, cooked crisp
Louis Dressing (recipe follows)
mixed spring greens
olive oil
sea salt

## Preparation

TOSS seafood, fruit, and prosciutto in a bowl with 4 ounces of Louis Dressing. Arrange on plates using a ring mold, and top with spring mix salad lightly dressed with olive oil and sea salt. Dress plates with additional Louis Dressing.

*Serves 2–4*

*Wine Suggestion: Pinot Grigio*

## For the Louis Dressing

1  cup mayonnaise
½  cup heavy cream

¼  cup sweet chili, strained
1  tablespoon lemon juice

COMBINE mayonnaise and cream in a mixer, whipping for 2 minutes. Using a fine mesh strainer, add sweet chili and lemon juice and combine.

# CRAB CAKES WITH SWEET PEPPER REMOULADE

## Ingredients

| | |
|---|---|
| 1 whole egg | ¼ cup sweet bell pepper, fine dice |
| ⅛ cup Dijon mustard | ¼ cup chives, sliced thin |
| ¼ cup mayonnaise | 1 pound Dungeness crabmeat |
| ½ teaspoon Tabasco® | 1 cup panko |
| 1 teaspoon Lea & Perrins | oil |
| 2 tablespoons lemon juice | Sweet Pepper Remoulade (recipe follows) |
| 1 teaspoon Old Bay Seasoning® | |
| ¼ cup red onion, fine dice | arugula or other bitter green salad mix |

## Preparation

MIX egg, mustard, Tabasco®, Lea & Perrins, lemon juice, and Old Bay Seasoning® in a bowl and set aside.

MAKE a brunoise of the onion and bell pepper by cooking them slowly in a small amount of butter. Add this brunoise to the bowl along with the chives. Add crabmeat and mix together gently. Then add breadcrumbs and gently mix again. Allow to sit for a minimum of 1 hour.

PREHEAT oven to 375 degrees. Shape crab mixture into 6 cakes and sear in a heavy-bottomed skillet in oil until brown. Flip cakes and place in oven to finish for about 5–7 minutes.

PLACE crab cakes on greens and serve with Sweet Pepper Remoulade.

### Yield: 6 4-ounce crab cakes

*Wine Suggestion: This can go several ways. Try a good quality Pinot Noir or Barnard Griffin Rosé of Sangiovese, Washington*

## For the Sweet Pepper Remoulade

| | |
|---|---|
| ½ cup mayonnaise | 1 teaspoon Worcestershire sauce |
| ⅛ cup roasted red peppers | ¼ teaspoon Old Bay Seasoning® |
| ⅛ cup red onions, diced | 1 tablespoon lemon juice |
| 1 teaspoon Tabasco® | |

PURÉE all ingredients in a food processor. Refrigerate for at least 1 hour before serving.

# The Wild Coho

THE WILD COHO

1044 Lawrence Street
Port Townsend, WA 98368
360-379-1030
www.thewildcoho.com

Dinner Tuesday through Saturday
from 4:30pm

# The Wild Coho

### *Jay Payne, Chef/Owner*
### *Christine Payne, Co-Owner*

"I believe that when a chef respects the ingredients, it shows in the meal." These words, from Chef Jay Payne, say it all about the quality of the cuisine that you will find at The Wild Coho, an intimate restaurant off the beaten path in Port Townsend. In 2000, Jay and his wife, Christine, moved to Port Townsend to pursue the dream of owning their own neighborhood restaurant. Jay works virtually alone in the kitchen, personally preparing every dish to ensure quality and consistency. In this way, Jay and Christine strive to keep a guest's experience at the restaurant as close to an invitation to dinner in their own home.

Jay's impressive resume includes eight years at Seattle's prestigious Four Seasons Olympic Hotel, where he worked with chefs from all over the world. After working in every area of the kitchen and rising to the rank of Chef de Cuisine of the Georgian Room, he left to open Tulio Ristorante in 1992 and helped establish it as *Seattle Magazine's* "Finest Italian Restaurant." Jay's artistry in the kitchen classified him in the ranks of those chefs who could truly succeed in the highly competitive world of Seattle cuisine. However, as Jay says, "Ever since the early eighties I've been eager to work directly with the producer in a 'farm-to-table' way." Port Townsend gave him the opportunity to do just that.

The mission of The Wild Coho is taken from the root of the word "restaurant," which comes from the French word "restaurer"—to restore. The Wild Coho's goal is to leave both its customers and the world a little better than it first found it. With 80% of its food local, organic, or both, the restaurant nurtures its guests with wholesome, healthy, and delicious foods that please the palate and also supports sustainable, locally grown products. The food that is prepared is frequently picked just hours before it is served. Chef Payne meets with the growers at the beginning of the planting season to discuss his needs. With the local Farmers' Market just across the street, it is a quick stop for the local growers on market days. You can also count on local and/or sustainably raised meats, local seafood, and of course, wild line-caught salmon. To complement your meal, you will find an affordable wine list focused on regional and sustainable wines and Jay's beautiful and decadent desserts.

# BAKED OYSTERS

*with Fennel and Preserved Lemon "Beurre-Blancandaise" Gratin*

## Ingredients

1 dozen oysters
rock salt
fresh fennel frond, for garnish

Preserved Lemon
"Beurre-Blancandaise" Gratin
(recipe follows)

## Preparation

PREHEAT oven to 400 degrees, and then switch to low broil. Carefully shuck oysters and place in a baking dish (a 'bed' of rock salt can help prevent them from tipping over). Top each oyster with a heaping tablespoon of Preserved Lemon "Beurre-Blancandaise Gratin and broil for 10–15 minutes, until golden brown. Present on a bed of fresh rock salt or on a cloth napkin garnished with fresh fennel frond.

*Serves 2 as an appetizer*

Wine Suggestion: *Generally, avoid oak-aged wines with oysters. A crisp Sauvignon Blanc, Pinot Gris, or sparkling wine would be wonderful.*

## For the Preserved Lemon "Beurre-Blancandaise" Gratin

⅓ cup white wine
zest and juice of 1 lemon
1 teaspoon shallot, very finely chopped
½ fennel bulb, small dice
¼ teaspoon ground fennel seed
¼ cup heavy cream
½ pound butter, chilled and cut into
small pieces

2 tablespoons preserved lemons, minced
2 tablespoons white wine vinegar
2 tablespoons lemon juice
3 egg yolks
1 tablespoon hot water
1 cup stiffly beaten whipped cream
(unsweetened)

BOIL wine, lemon juice and zest, shallot, and fennel bulb and ground fennel in a heavy stainless (or other non-reactive) medium saucepan over medium-high heat until reduced to almost dry. Add cream and reduce until thickened. Reduce heat to medium-low and whisk in butter, one piece at a time. Add pieces before the previous ones have completely emulsified. When all of the butter has been whisked in, add the preserved lemon and place in a warm location while you make the hollandaise.

IN A small mixing bowl, whisk together vinegar, lemon juice, and yolks. Place over a pan of simmering water (medium-high heat) and whisk constantly as the sauce thickens. Continue whisking and cooking only until the whisk exposes the bottom of the bowl as you stir. Remove from heat and whisk in the tablespoon of hot water. Slowly drizzle and whisk in the warm butter sauce until completely blended into the egg mixture. Allow to cool to room temperature and then fold in whipped cream. This mixture can be prepared up to two days in advance.

# SWEET POTATO CRUSTED SALMON
## *with Green Onion Butter and Tomato Relish*

## Ingredients

4  6-ounce salmon fillet
4  medium sweet potatoes, julienne
   vegetable oil

Tomato Relish (recipe follows)
Green Onion Butter (recipe follows)

## Preparation

PREHEAT oven to 450 degrees. Pre-heat a non-stick pan (with an oven-proof handle) with ¼ inch of vegetable oil over medium-high heat until the oil just begins to smoke.

CAREFULLY place a small handful of julienned potato in the pan, about the size of your fillet of salmon. Carefully place salmon fillet on the pile of sweet potato. Allow potato to brown slightly and place pan in oven on bottom rack. Cook until salmon is nearly cooked through with some translucent area remaining, about 4 minutes. Check frequently to avoid over-browning the potatoes. Carefully remove from pan and invert onto plate or paper towel to drain. Place on plate and garnish with a heaping tablespoon of Tomato Relish and a table-spoon of the Green Onion Butter.

### *Serves 4*

*Wine Suggestion: A dry Riesling, an off-dry Gewürztraminer, or even a Pinot Noir*

## For the Tomato Relish

½  onion, peeled, diced
   vegetable oil
2  tablespoons sugar
½  teaspoon curry powder
¼  cup red wine vinegar

1  28-ounce can diced tomato
⅛  teaspoon cinnamon
¼  teaspoon thyme
¼  teaspoon sumac (optional)
   freshly ground black pepper

SAUTÉ the onion in a medium non-reactive saucepan over medium heat in a bit of vegetable oil. Add sugar and curry powder and lightly 'fry'. Add red wine vinegar and reduce to nearly dry. Add diced tomato and simmer 20 minutes over low heat. Add seasonings to taste. Cool thoroughly.

## For the Green Onion Butter

6 *green onions, cleaned*
½ *stick (2 ounces) butter, softened*
4 *tablespoons white wine*

1 *tablespoon heavy cream*
4 *tablespoons vegetable stock*

CUT green onion into roughly ½-inch pieces. Blanch for only about 5 seconds in rapidly boiling salted water. Cool thoroughly and quickly in ice water. Purée in blender with a splash of cold water to keep it moving in the blender. In a food processor, spin softened butter. Slowly add the green onion mixture until completely blended. (This compound butter can be made ahead and even frozen for future use). In a small non-reactive pan combine remaining ingredients and reduce to a thick, cream-like consistency over medium high heat. Reduce heat to low and whisk in the green onion/butter mixture, piece by piece until completely incorporated into a sauce. Thin the sauce with warm water or vegetable stock, if necessary. Season to taste with salt and pepper. Keep in a warm place until ready for use.

*Sweet Potato Crusted Salmon*

# SWEET POTATO GNOCCHI
*with Brown Butter and Sage*

At Wild Coho, we serve these with crème fraîche or fromage blanc and shaved Parmigiano Grana Padano. Sour cream is an acceptable substitute and any good quality Parmesan, Romano, or Manchego would be great.

## Ingredients

3 pounds sweet potatoes (not yams)
1 egg, beaten
2 cups all-purpose flour (approximately)
½ teaspoon salt
¼ teaspoon pepper
1 tablespoon butter – per each dozen gnocchi

½ teaspoon fresh sage, chopped – per each dozen gnocchi
crème fraîche or fromage blanc
shaved Parmigiano Grana Padano

## Preparation

IN A large stockpot bring sweet potatoes and cold water to a boil, reduce to a simmer and cook until the potatoes are soft throughout—approximately one 1 hour—depending on the size of the potatoes (test by poking with a knife).

PREHEAT oven to 350 degrees. Drain off potatoes, place on baking sheet and bake for 15–20 minutes to dry them slightly. Remove from oven and let cool until they can be handled. Peel potatoes and press through a potato ricer. Add the beaten egg and 1½ cups flour, salt, and pepper. Gently fold together—just enough to mix in the flour. It is vital that the dough not be over-mixed and stirred. Handle gently. Fold in ½ cup flour and check the dough for wetness; it should begin to feel more like a paste/dough and offer some resistance when poked. Adjust with more flour as necessary. Allow the dough to rest for 10 minutes.

LIGHTLY dust a cutting board with flour. Scoop out approximately 1 cup of the dough and roll into a cylinder-shaped rope, about ½ to ¾ inch in diameter. Cut into 1-inch long pieces and set aside. Gnocchi can be stored up to 2 days in this form, on a baking sheet dusted with semolina, in the refrigerator.

BRING a large pot of salted water to boil. In a non-stick skillet, melt 1 teaspoon butter per dozen gnocchi you will be cooking and allow to brown slightly. Drop gnocchi into water and cook at a simmer until at least one gnocchi begins to float. Remove gnocchi from water and carefully add to skillet with the browned butter. Panfry over medium-high heat to brown on both sides and add ½ teaspoon of chopped fresh sage (per each dozen).

*Serves 5–7*

# Bella Italia

**Bella Italia**

118 E. 1st Street   Dinner nightly from 4:00pm
Port Angeles, WA 98362
360-457-5442
www.bellaitaliapa.com

# Bella Italia

### *Neil Conklin, Proprietor*
### *Dave Senters, Chef*

Port Angeles has been a vigorous harbor for trade and commerce for almost 150 years. A Custom House was established here in 1861 and, in 1862, Abraham Lincoln issued an executive order establishing Port Angeles as a town site—the only other executive order of this type was issued to establish Washington, D.C. Most of the land was held as a military reserve until 1894, when the U.S. Congress agreed to the sale of lots. The town prospered over the years with the forest and fishing industries. The regenerative forest around Port Angeles supplied the building materials for Seattle and San Francisco, and the massive logs were shipped through the port. The salmon in the Strait were very plentiful and boats from the harbor, both commercial and private, easily caught their limits.

Today, located just a couple blocks from the busy harbor, is a delightful Italian restaurant that offers modern Italian regional cuisine with Olympic Coast ingredients. The Italian regions represented in the fare are those with some climatic and culinary connections to the Port Angeles area, namely the northern and coastal Italian regions. Some of the farms in the rich Dungeness Valley agricultural area contribute to the restaurant's cuisine, and the healthy local runs of steelhead and salmon add their flavorful tastes to the menu.

Bella Italia has a notable wine program, which has been recognized by the *Wine Spectator* magazine with its *Award of Excellence*. The restaurant carries over 600 selections, leaning toward Washington, the West Coast, and of course, Italy. Various food and wine events with partner wineries are featured in the winter months, and a pairing menu is offered year round.

Chef Dave Senters started with Bella Italia eight years ago, after working in the Seattle culinary scene at such venues as Reiners, The Lakeside, and The Warwick Hotel. Dave's training has been from the ground up, supplemented with classes at the Culinary Institute of America at Greystone and in Italy, at Toscana Saporita. While in Italy on a "fact finding" mission to learn about the Tenuta Castello rice used at the restaurant, he worked with chefs specializing in risotto. He also did a demonstration at the Vinitaly wine fair in Verona, featuring the risotto from the farm with red wine from the famous southern Piedmont region.

Both Neil and Dave stay active promoting a regional food economy with the goal of growing the demand for locally produced food. Neil achieves this goal through farmers' markets, local festivals, and by bringing the producers into the restaurant to meet the consumers.

 Award of Excellence

# NASH HUBER'S CAULIFLOWER
## *with Raisins and Pine Nuts*

Every culture seems to have a version of a sweet and sour dish. This is quite tame, in that the sweet and sour are derived only from lemon zest and raisins, as I prefer it. Nash Huber's Dungeness Valley farm has supplied the restaurant with cauliflower and other produce since its beginning. -Dave Senters, Chef

## Ingredients

1  medium-sized head cauliflower
6  tablespoons unsalted butter
1  tablespoon garlic, finely minced
¾  cup raisins
½  cup toasted pine nuts

2  tablespoons flat leaf parsley, roughly
   chopped
1  lemon
   salt & pepper

## Preparation

CUT cauliflower into bite-size chunks. From the top, cut into 4 symmetrical quarters, and carve off the stem. In a large pot of boiling water, blanch the cauliflower for 2–3 minutes. Drain and cool under cold running water. Set aside.

IN A large skillet heat the butter on medium heat until it has completely melted and become a bit foamy. Continue heating, watching carefully, until foam disappears and butter becomes a light brown color. Pull off heat immediately.

ADD cauliflower and garlic to butter and return to low heat. Add raisins and pine nuts and simmer until cauliflower is heated through, about 2–3 more minutes. Add parsley and, with a box grater, zest the lemon into the pan. Add salt and pepper to preference and serve.

### *Serves 4 as appetizer or side dish*

*Beverage Suggestion: You could drink an inexpensive picnic-type white wine with this or hard apple cider is good, especially if you want to ramp up the sweet and sour on a "splash for the cauliflower and a splash for me" basis.*

# OLIVE OIL POACHED ALBACORE TUNA
## with Red Wine Risotto

Salmon would work well with this, but tuna is traditional and combines well with red wine. We made this (without the tuna) as a risotto cooking demonstration for Tenuta Castello farms at Vinitaly. Some recipes say not to add wine until last, to prevent its acidity from toughening the rice. In Italy they added it first, and I never noticed a difference. This recipe would serve four as a main course but can be adjusted upward remembering to "not crowd the pan".

## Ingredients

- 3 cups olive oil, approximately (regular olive oil, labeled "Pure Olive Oil" in the supermarket)
- 2 bulbs garlic (about 10 cloves), peeled
- 4 bay leaves
- 1 teaspoon black peppercorns
- 2 8-ounce Albacore tuna filets
- 8 cups roasted vegetable stock, (can substitute a good store-bought stock base)
- ¼ cup bacon, preferably pancetta, minced

- ½ cup onion, finely chopped
- 1 cup mushrooms, chanterelles if available, sliced
- 1½ cups dry red wine
- 1 teaspoon thyme, fresh or dried
- 2 cups Carnaroli, Arborio, or similar rice
- 3 ounces butter
- ¾ cup grated Parmesan cheese
  salt & pepper to taste

## Preparation

IN A large flat skillet heat the olive oil and garlic cloves to about 180 degrees for about 30–45 minutes. If a thermometer is not available the oil should be watched carefully to ensure it does not get too hot, as evidenced by telltale bubbles as the garlic begins to fry. Cook the garlic slowly, until it starts to become soft and mushy, about 40 minutes. When it reaches this consistency, remove the garlic cloves with a fork or slotted spoon, and set aside to be used with the risotto. Add bay leaves and peppercorns to the oil.

SALT the tuna and place in the oil; the oil should cover the fish. Watch the fish carefully. When gray on the outside but still fairly pink and opaque in the center, remove from the oil and set aside.

IN A saucepan bring the vegetable stock to a simmer on a back burner. Heat a large heavy-bottomed saucepan on a front burner. Add bacon and stir, frying until the fat begins to render. Add onions and mushrooms, and sauté with the bacon for 1 minute, then add the red wine, the saved "roasted" garlic, and the thyme. Reduce the wine by at least half.

ADD the rice to the red wine saucepan. With a ladle, add simmering stock to the rice from the saucepan on the back burner. Begin stirring the rice constantly, adding more simmering stock in increments as it is absorbed into the rice. After 17–20 minutes of stirring and adding liquid, the rice grains should be creamy and soft. Stir in the butter and Parmesan cheese. Adjust the seasoning with salt and pepper.

TO SERVE, tear the tuna into bite-size chunks, fold into the rice and serve.

### Serves 4

*Wine Suggestion: Try this with Washington Sangiovese, (our favorite: Walla Walla Vintners), or a Valpolicella.*

# WHITE KING SALMON
*with Sundried Tomato Pink Peppercorn Butter*

Learned this at "Peters on the Park" restaurant in Madison Park years ago. The smoky, piquant combination seems to accentuate oily-meaty fish like salmon, tuna, and sturgeon, especially when barbequed or grilled. This is versatile in that it would be a fine counterpoint to a salad, perhaps served cold, or as a main course.

## Ingredients

¾ packed cup sundried tomatoes (dry or packed in oil—see note in preparation)

8 ounces (1stick) butter

¼ cup pink peppercorns

1 heaping tablespoon flat leaf parsley, rough chopped

1 heaping tablespoon shallot, rough chopped

4 8-ounce white king salmon filets, (or other salmon, tuna, etc.)
vegetable oil
salt & pepper to taste

## Preparation

IF the tomatoes are purchased dry—rather than packed in oil—they should be re-hydrated by soaking in hot water for 1 hour or more, till quite soft and "mushy".

SOFTEN butter 15 to 30 seconds in the microwave. In a food processor add the softened butter, the drained sundried tomatoes, and the pink peppercorns, and pulse for 15–30 seconds, scraping down the sides of the processor bowl. Add parsley and shallots, and perhaps a pinch of salt (if butter is unsalted) and fresh grated black pepper. Pulse until combined. If a food processor is unavailable, all the dry and drained ingredients can be very finely chopped and worked into the softened butter. This is not a cold "compound" butter, but should be kept warm, and used immediately. Any extra butter is very good with grilled vegetables, such as zucchini, onions, and peppers.

PREHEAT grill or barbeque. Oil, salt, and pepper the salmon, and place skin side up on hot grill or barbeque. The skin side will be the flatter of the two sides on a filet. With a "steak cut" salmon or tuna, this is not important. Allow the salmon to cook under a medium to high heat for 3–6 minutes depending on thickness, then turn the fish over and baste with the sundried peppercorn butter until fish is ready to serve, being careful not to overcook.

*Serves 4*

*Wine Suggestion: This dish needs a white wine with full-bodied ripeness and acidity, a Chardonnay or Pinot Grigio from the Alto Adige in northern Italy, or any of a wide variety of Sauvignon Blanc-based wines.*

# ROASTED LAMB SIRLOIN
## *with Mint Gremolata*

Lamb sirloin can be a bit difficult to find, but is an inexpensive and flavorful alternative to rack of lamb. Check with your grocer or online. It will come in a two- to four-pound roast that will have a bit of a fat cap on one side that can be easily trimmed off; or your butcher may "trim and tie" it for you. In any case, it makes a good spring or fall comfort food type dish.

## Ingredients

- ½ cup brown sugar
- 3 tablespoons kosher salt
- ⅓ cup dried mushrooms (chanterelles, shitakes, or porcini, whatever is in your grocery store), finely ground in a clean coffee grinder
- 3 tablespoons garlic, finely minced
- 1 tablespoon black pepper, ground

- 1 tablespoon dried rosemary, coarsely ground in a clean coffee grinder
  olive oil
- 1 2- to 4-pound lamb sirloin
- ¼ cup red wine
- 1 pat of butter
  Mint Gremolata (recipe follows)

## Preparation

COMBINE the sugar, salt, mushroom powder, garlic, pepper, and rosemary in a large bowl. While stirring, add just enough olive oil to form a wet paste. Coat the trimmed lamb all over with the paste and refrigerate overnight.

PREHEAT the oven to 375 degrees. Place the lamb in a large shallow-sided metal pot and roast for 40–50 minutes, or until a meat thermometer registers an internal temperature of 120 degrees for medium rare. When done, allow to rest for 10 minutes before serving.

THE lamb cooking pot will contain a "jus" given off by the cooking lamb that can be served with it. Add red wine and butter to the "jus" and then cook on the stovetop over high heat for 2–3 minutes while stirring.

TO SERVE, thinly slice the lamb and place on plates. Drizzle a little of the red wine sauce over the lamb and sprinkle the Mint Gremolata evenly over all.

### *Serves 4 to 8, depending on size of sirloin*

*Wine Suggestion: Serve with Washington Syrah or Cabernet.*

## For the Mint Gremolata

- ¼ cup packed fresh mint leaves, coarsely chopped
- 2 lemons, grated or zested into julienne strips
- 5 cloves garlic, very thinly sliced

COMBINE the mint, lemon zest, and garlic loosely by hand, and set aside for service.

# Heintz Farm Blackberry Cocktail

Almost everyone who grew up in the Northwest remembers a favorite vacant lot where jungles of blackberry vines grew. At the restaurant we use Dan Heintz's Chester varietal, which has a thornless cane and fewer seeds in the fruit. This "cocktail" is a blackberry mousse that makes a light dessert. Note: Pasteurized eggs or egg whites are available at most grocers, if using raw egg white is a concern to you.

## Ingredients

> 1 *quart fresh or frozen blackberries*
> 1½ *cups sugar*
> 1 *envelope (1¾ teaspoons) unflavored gelatin*
> ¼ *cup cold water*
>
> 3 *eggs, separated (save yolks for another use)*
> 1 *cup whipping cream*
> *fresh berries and mint, for garnish*

## Preparation

IN A medium saucepan heat the berries and sugar to a simmer. Pull from heat and strain into a large mixing bowl, mashing the berries with a spatula or spoon to extract the pulp.

IN A small container, (a coffee cup is perfect) bloom the gelatin by pouring the powder into the cup and add the cold water. Stir until dissolved and let sit. In a couple minutes the gelatin will have hardened. Melt the gelatin in the microwave for 15 seconds. It will liquefy again. Add to the warm berry and sugar mixture.

BEAT the egg whites in a dry grease-free bowl until they turn opaque, begin to thicken, and look foamy. Beat until they form soft peaks and look shiny, but not too firm, 3–4 minutes. In a separate bowl, whip the cream until it develops firm peaks.

COOL the berry mixture to room temperature by whisking over ice water, or cool in the refrigerator. Add half the whipped egg whites, folding in with a spatula. Add the remaining egg whites. Add the whipped cream in increments, folding in until combined. Spoon the mousse into cocktail glasses, refrigerate for at least 4 hours, but serve within 1 or 2 days. Serve garnished with mint and fresh berries.

*Serves 6*

# Toga's

## TOGA'S
### NORTHWEST & INTERNATIONAL CUISINE

122 W. Lauridsen Blvd.  Dinner Tuesday through
Port Angeles, WA 98362  Saturday from 5:00pm
360-452-1952

# Toga's

### *Toga Hertzog, Executive Chef/Co-owner*
### *Lisa Hertzog, Manager, Co-owner*

Inside the teal-colored shingled house on West Lauridsen Boulevard in Port Angeles awaits a unique dining experience for the curious gourmet. The mission of the owners, Toga and Lisa Hertzog, is to offer fine food in a relaxed atmosphere, with time for the guest to enjoy each course and with a waitstaff that is attentive, but willing to work at each guest's pace.

A native of Port Angeles, Toga grew up with wanderlust. Shortly after high school graduation, Toga enrolled in a culinary program in the Black Forest region of Germany. As part of the program, he apprenticed at German hotels in the region. Upon graduation, Toga joined the fine dining restaurant at the Royal Waikoloa Hotel in Hawaii, where he learned the fine points of the Asian and Pacific Rim style of cuisine. His next education came as a Chef de Rotisserie and Chef de Poissonier aboard the Royal Viking Sun cruise ship, where he met his future wife, Lisa.

After several tours aboard ship, Toga brought Lisa home to Port Angeles to visit, and they immediately decided to live there. After working at the Chestnut Cottage restaurant, Toga decided to set up his own restaurant and opened Toga's, specializing in Northwest and International Cuisine. His immersion in Pacific Rim cooking gave him a love of fresh local produce, and the seafood that comes right out of Neah Bay. His German culinary education provided him with unique cooking techniques that are especially enjoyed by his customers. A variety of fondues are offered, from the traditional cheese fondue to broths for cooking vegetables and meats.

However, the most unique cuisine offered at Toga's is the Jagerstein, a method of cooking with very hot stones—a German tradition developed centuries ago by rangers who managed the game on the German estates. At Toga's, the food is pre-prepped and brought to the table raw. Special stones are used that have been tested for food compatibility—many stones, when heated to high temperatures, give off smells and emissions that could negatively impact the food. Lisa and Toga have brought back tested sets of these stones from Germany. The stones are slowly heated to 500 degrees, placed on a tray, and brought to the table. The guests have the option to cook their own combination of foods on the stone, with a variety of sauces provided to increase the dining options. A nicely balanced wine list features California and Northwest wineries with a smattering of wines from around the world.

# Hungarian Goulash Soup

A hearty winter soup that will satisfy any appetite, the beef tenderloin adds great flavor and melts in your mouth.

## Ingredients

2  tablespoons canola oil
1  pound fresh end trimmings from beef tenderloin, cut into ¼-inch cubes
1  tablespoon (2 large) shallots, chopped
1  tablespoon (3 large cloves) garlic, chopped
1  large jumbo yellow onion, finely diced
1½  cups (or 15 ounces) tomato paste
5  cups beef stock
½  teaspoon ground cumin
2  teaspoons Hungarian paprika

2  cups green, yellow, and/or red bell peppers, finely diced (¼-inch)
1  large potato, cubed
1  tablespoon all-purpose flour
1  teaspoon sugar
pinch  salt
fresh white pepper, cracked
⅓  cup port
1  tablespoon fresh tarragon, chopped
chopped fresh parsley, for garnish

## Preparation

PLACE canola oil in medium saucepan and sear beef tenderloin cubes on high heat for 5 minutes. Add shallots, garlic, and onions and sauté until golden in color. Add tomato paste, beef stock, cumin, paprika, bell peppers, potatoes, and flour. Bring to a rolling simmer for about 1 hour, until the soup thickens. Add sugar, salt, and pepper to taste. Stir in port and tarragon and simmer for 15 more minutes. Sprinkle chopped parsley on top for garnish.

### Serves 6–8

*Wine Suggestion: a big luscious red wine such as a Camaraderie Malbec would be a phenomenal pairing with this soup.*

# Northwest Seafood Chowder

The preparation of this soup is time consuming, but the final reward is well worth it. All the flavors of the sea combine to make this much-requested chowder a delicious feast in itself. Of course, a fresh baked San Francisco style sourdough baguette would really make this dish complete!

## Ingredients

⅓ cup salted butter
⅓ cup onion, finely diced
⅓ cup celery, finely diced
⅓ cup red bell pepper, finely diced
2 tablespoons fresh garlic, chopped
2 tablespoons fresh ginger, chopped
2 cups red potato, finely diced
⅓ cup flour
6 prawns with shell on (16/20 count)
1½ cups white wine (preferably Chablis)
10 fresh Manila clams
20 fresh Penn Cove mussels
3 cups heavy cream

6 ounces fresh king salmon, cubed
6 ounces fresh halibut, cubed
6 ounces Atlantic sea scallops (30/40 count)
¼ cup cream sherry
salt
sugar
Old Bay Seasoning®
fresh dill, chopped
fresh black pepper, cracked
cayenne pepper to taste
fresh tarragon, chopped (optional)

## Preparation

MELT butter in a medium-sized saucepan and add onions, celery, bell peppers, garlic, potatoes, and ginger. Sauté for about 2 minutes and then dust the mixture with the flour. Set aside.

PEEL prawns and cut them in half. Boil shells in white wine for 1–2 minutes. Strain liquid into another pan, discard shells, and add clams and mussels to liquid. Bring to a boil and cook until all the shells open, about 1–2 minutes. Discard any shells that have not opened. Remove clam and mussel meat from opened shells and set aside. Strain wine stock and add to the sautéed vegetables. Add heavy cream, a pinch of dill, sugar, salt, Old Bay Seasoning® and cracked pepper. Bring everything to a rolling boil and simmer on medium heat until potatoes are almost soft. Add salmon, halibut, scallops, and peeled prawns and simmer until seafood is cooked. Add clams and mussels.

FINISH off with cream sherry and cayenne pepper. Add salt or sugar to taste, as desired. Let chowder sit, covered, for 10 minutes to let all the flavors come together. Ladle into bowls and garnish with fresh chopped dill or tarragon.

### Serves 6

*Wine Suggestions: A clean, crisp Sémillon or Chardonnay, perhaps an Australian Penfold's Coonawara would be just the right touch to add to this wonderful chowder.*

# CREAM OF TOMATO SOUP

This soup has become a house favorite among guests. The balsamic vinegar and sherry just add a little extra kick that intensifies the tomato flavor.

## Ingredients

1 tablespoon (2 large) shallots, chopped
1 tablespoon (3 large cloves) garlic, chopped
1 tablespoon extra virgin olive oil
1½ cups (or 15 ounces) tomato paste
1 cup chicken stock
4 cups heavy whipping cream

2 tablespoons balsamic vinegar
1 teaspoon sugar
pinch salt, to taste
⅓ cup cream sherry
1 tablespoon basil, chopped (plus extra for garnish)

## Preparation

IN A medium saucepan, sauté shallots and garlic in olive oil until golden in color. Add tomato paste, chicken stock, cream, and balsamic vinegar. Bring to a rolling simmer for about 10–15 minutes, until soup thickens. Add sugar and salt to taste, stir in sherry and basil and simmer for 5 more minutes.

LADLE into bowls and garnish with chopped basil. For an extra touch, whip a little heavy whipping cream in a mixer with a splash of sherry and spoon a teaspoon onto soup before serving.

### Serves 6

*Wine Suggestion: A crisp Pinot Grigio, such as Riff from Italy, would be a nice accompaniment.*

# Macadamia Coconut Crusted King Salmon
## with Orange Soy Caramel Glaze and Ginger Beurre Blanc

This dish brings a little "Northwest–Hawaiian" fusion into our house menu. It is simply one of my favorite ways to prepare fresh Northwest king salmon. The nuts give a great texture and the combination of sauces just explode with flavor! This is especially good served on a bed of steamed rice.

## Ingredients

| | |
|---|---|
| 6 8-ounce fresh king salmon filets | 1 cup all-purpose flour |
| 10 ounces Macadamia nuts, chopped | ½ cup peanut oil, for sautéing |
| 4 ounces unsweetened coconut flakes | Ginger Beurre Blanc (recipe follows) |
| salt & pepper to taste | Orange Soy Caramel Glaze |
| 2 eggs, lightly whipped | (recipe follows) |

## Preparation

PREHEAT oven to 350 degrees. Set up three small trays for dipping. Place flour in first tray, whipped eggs in second tray, and macadamia nuts and coconut in third tray. Season salmon filets with salt and pepper and then dip each one—flesh side down—in flour, then egg mix, and then in nut mix.

HEAT sauté pan with peanut oil to medium heat and place fish into pan, nut side down. Sauté for 1–2 minutes, until crust is golden brown. Be careful not to blacken the crust. Turn fish over and continue cooking on other side. Put on a baking sheet and finish in oven for 2–3 minutes, depending on thickness of fish.

TO SERVE, lay each filet on a bed of steamed rice. Ladle some Ginger Beurre Blanc around the fish and ladle some Orange Soy Caramel Glaze over the fish and into the ginger sauce.

*Serves 6*

*Wine Suggestion: A smooth reserve Ferrari Carrano Chardonnay would be an elegant wine for this dish.*

## For the Ginger Beurre Blanc Sauce

| | |
|---|---|
| 2 cups heavy cream | 1 tablespoon sugar |
| 4 tablespoons fresh ginger, chopped | pinch salt |
| 2 tablespoons rice wine vinegar | 1 cup unsalted butter, cut in small pieces |

PLACE all ingredients except butter in a medium saucepan and bring to a rolling simmer, then reduce for about 10 minutes. Let cool down and slowly mix in pieces of butter with a mixing wand or hand mixer until sauce thickens. Add salt and sugar to taste and keep warm for service.

## For Orange Soy Caramel Glaze

| | |
|---|---|
| 1 cup sugar | 2 cups fresh squeezed orange juice |
| 1 cup rice wine vinegar | 2 tablespoons garlic, chopped |
| 1 cup soy sauce | 2 tablespoons fresh ginger, chopped |
| 1 teaspoon crushed chili flakes | slurry of cornstarch and water |

PLACE all ingredients except slurry in a medium saucepan and bring to a boil. Simmer for about 10–15 minutes. Thicken with a slurry of cornstarch and water. Keep warm for service.

# NEAH BAY BAKED HALIBUT
## *with Dungeness Crab and Garlic Herb Crust*

This is the classic Northwest dish, a true crowd pleaser every time. The halibut is so subtle and offers an unbelievable texture, while the Dungeness crab and garlic herb crust highlight the fish. A longstanding seasonal favorite of our guests, we usually serve this with a wild rice pilaf and fresh oven-roasted asparagus. Be sure to make the Garlic Herb Crust several hours before you start the rest of the dish.

## Ingredients

4  cups white wine, such as Chablis
4  cups fish stock
3½  pounds fresh Northwest halibut filet,
    cut in 8-ounce portions
    salt and pepper to taste

1½  pounds fresh Dungeness crabmeat
    Garlic Herb Crust (recipe follows)
    Note: Be sure to make first
½  cup shallots, chopped

## Preparation

PREHEAT convection oven to 375 degrees. Mix white wine and fish stock. Pour a little of this mixture into a metal sheet pan that has a rim. Lightly salt and pepper the halibut filets and lay the steaks onto the sheet pan. Top with crabmeat. Slice the chilled block of Garlic Herb Crust into thin strips and place onto the seafood. Fill sheet pan ¼ way with the wine and stock mix and sprinkle the chopped shallots around the halibut. Bake in convection oven for about 15–20 minutes, or until fish is cooked to desired temperature.

### *Serves 6*

*Wine Suggestion: A full-bodied Chardonnay, such as Newton unfiltered Napa Valley, would be great with this dish.*

## For the Garlic Herb Crust

2  pounds salted butter
2  tablespoons fresh garlic, chopped
4  large eggs
¼  cup (total) mix of fresh parsley,
    oregano, and basil, chopped
    sugar, salt, cayenne pepper, and fresh
    cracked pepper to taste

1  cup Jarlsberg cheese, grated
1  cup Romano cheese, grated
2  cups Japanese panko breadcrumbs
splash brandy

IN A mixer, place butter and chopped garlic and whip slowly until smooth. Slowly add eggs, one at a time. Then add the herbs along with the sugar, salt, cayenne pepper and fresh cracked pepper to taste. Add grated cheese and lightly fold in the panko and brandy—the panko with soak up the brandy. Form into a block, wrap in plastic wrap, and chill in refrigerator for 2–3 hours until hard.

# Lake Cresent Lodge

**LAKE CRESCENT LODGE**

416 Lake Crescent Road
Port Angeles, WA 98363
360-928-3211 Ext. 17
www.foreverlodging.com

Breakfast: 7:30am – 10:00am
Lunch: Noon – 2:30pm
Dinner: 6:00pm – 9:00pm
Dinner reservations required

# Lake Crescent Lodge

### Gary Wood, General Manager
### Jim Stanley, Executive Chef

Lake Crescent Lodge was built in 1916, as Singer's Tavern, on a clearing at Barnes Point. Al Singer originally intended it as a sportsman's lodge, along with numerous other unique resorts around the shores of the newly discovered Lake Crescent. His guests came to enjoy the spectacular views and warm themselves by the baronial fireplace in the rustic, but cozy, tavern.

Lake Crescent Tavern, as it was known at the time, played an important role in the final decision to designate much of the Olympic Peninsula as a national park. Following the urging of local dignitaries and citizens, President Franklin D. Roosevelt visited the area in 1937. He arrived in Port Angeles Harbor by ship and then traveled to Lake Crescent by motorcar to spend some time studying the area and consider his decision to create Olympic National Park. For the night of September 30, 1937 Lake Crescent Tavern became the American White House. After spending the night in a cabin just southwest of the tavern, the President enjoyed a hearty breakfast of fresh trout that had been caught for him in Barnes Creek.

Most of the original resorts around Lake Crescent have been lost over time. But Lake Crescent Lodge has continued the tradition of service and hospitality for which Al Singer, and others that followed him, became famous. The lodge has hosted numerous congressmen, senators, cabinet secretaries, and such well-known guests as Supreme Court Justice William O. Douglas, U.S. Attorney General Robert Kennedy, and First Lady Laura Bush. The hospitality that the lodge has shown to such famous guests is also provided to the ordinary visitor, making a stop here a must if visiting the park.

Dining at Lake Crescent Lodge is a very pleasurable experience. Guests can relax in the expansive Sun Room, or outside in Adirondack chairs, and watch the sun set over the lake while enjoying a beverage from the lodge's extensive wine and spirits list. The lodge promotes wines from award-winning Pacific Northwest wine regions, and has been awarded the *Washington Wine First Award for Fine Dining* by the Washington State Wine Commission and the *Seattle Post Intelligencer*. Inside the lodge, guests will enjoy a casual family atmosphere in which to appreciate the fine cuisine produced in the lodge's kitchen. Forever Resorts, who owns the lodge, embraces a philosophy of providing sustainable, local, and organic products for their cuisine, resulting in flavorful meals with a special freshness.

# DUNGENESS CRAB CAKES
## with Blood Orange Sauce and Capers

## Ingredients

1  red pepper, diced
1  green pepper, diced
1  red onion, diced
   olive oil
1  pound fresh Dungeness crabmeat
3  eggs
8  ounces Parmesan cheese, grated
½  teaspoon salt
½  teaspoon pepper
¼  teaspoon red pepper flakes

1  tablespoon dry thyme leaves
2  ounces fresh garlic, chopped
1  quart heavy cream
2  ounces green onion, diced
8  ounces panko breadcrumbs, plus extra
   for coating
6  ounces spring mix or arugula
   Blood Orange Sauce (recipe follows)
1  ounce capers

## Preparation

SAUTÉ peppers and red onion in a small amount of olive oil on high heat until al dente. Set aside and let cool, then refrigerate. In a large mixing bowl add Dungeness crabmeat, eggs, Parmesan, salt, pepper, red pepper flakes, thyme leaves, and fresh garlic. Add in the cooled peppers and onion and combine well. Next add the heavy cream until mixture is loose. Add green onions and panko, mix together and let sit in the refrigerator for 2 hours.

FORM crabmeat mixture into 2-ounce portions and roll in panko to coat the outside. Let crab cakes sit in the refrigerator to set up for ½ hour.

HEAT a griddle or skillet to 350 degrees. Add a little canola oil and brown both sides of the crab cakes until middle is hot. On a plate, place the spring mix and /or arugula in the center of the plate. Rest one or two of the crab cakes on the spring mix, then squeeze Blood Orange Sauce on or around the crab cakes and sprinkle capers on top and serve.

### Serves 6

*Wine Suggestion: Try a Chardonnay with citrus flavors*

## For the Blood Orange Sauce

6  ounces blood orange purée
2  ounces superfine sugar

1  ounce cornstarch slurry

HEAT up the blood orange purée and sugar mixture in a saucepan on medium-high heat. Once the sauce comes to a boil, taste to make sure it is not too tart. Add extra sugar if necessary. Whisk in the cornstarch slurry until thick. Pour through a mesh strainer and let cool in the refrigerator. After sauce has cooled, put into a squeeze bottle for storage until service.

# SEARED SCALLOP AND ESCAROLE SALAD
### with Bleu Cheese Vinaigrette and Roasted Sweet Potatoes

## Ingredients

2 sweet potatoes, peeled and diced
olive oil
salt & pepper to taste
1½ pounds fresh large diver sea scallops

2 heads escarole, cut in half
Bleu Cheese Vinaigrette
(recipe follows)

## Preparation

PREHEAT oven to 350 degrees. Toss potatoes in a bowl with a small amount of olive oil, salt, and pepper. Lay the potatoes on a sheet pan and roast in oven for about 20 minutes or until tender. Set aside and cover with foil.

HEAT a non-stick sauté pan on high and add 1 ounce of olive oil. Salt and pepper the scallops to taste and sear on both sides evenly for about 4 minutes. The scallops should feel springy to the touch. Set aside.

WASH and dry the escarole halves thoroughly. Place each half on a plate with the cut side up and place warm sweet potatoes around the outside. Heat up the Bleu Cheese Vinaigrette enough to melt the cheese, dress salad lightly, and place the seared scallops on top.

### Serves 4

*Wine Suggestion: A light rosé, such as Three Rivers, Walla Walla, WA*

## For the Bleu Cheese Vinaigrette

1 cup red wine vinegar
1 tablespoon Dijon mustard
½ cup brown sugar
pinch salt

¼ teaspoon fresh ground pepper
1 cup olive oil
1 cup canola oil
¾ cup bleu cheese

IN A food processor, combine red wine vinegar, Dijon mustard, brown sugar, salt, pepper and mix until well blended. Combine the olive and canola oils in a separate container and drizzle them slowly into the running food processor until thoroughly incorporated. Crumble the bleu cheese and add to the dressing by hand.

# BAKED KING SALMON
*with Smoked Salmon Horseradish Crust, Sweet Potato Pommes Frites, and Beurre Blanc*

## Ingredients

| | |
|---|---|
| 1 | 6-ounce piece of smoked wild salmon |
| ½ | cup breadcrumbs |
| pinch | fresh ground black pepper |
| ½ | cup horseradish root, freshly shredded |
| 1 | cup scallions, sliced ⅛-inch thick |
| 2 | 6-ounce fillets of fresh king salmon, pin bones removed |

1   large sweet potato, peeled and halved into ⅛-inch julienne slices
vegetable oil for frying
Beurre Blanc (recipe follows)
fresh spring asparagus and chives for garnish

## Preparation

PREHEAT oven to 400 degrees. Combine smoked salmon, breadcrumbs, and pepper, and chop in food processor (not too fine). Place into a mixing bowl and add shredded horseradish root and scallions. Mix together. Place the two 6-ounce king salmon fillets on baking sheet. Add a thick layer of smoked salmon crust on top and place in oven. Bake until salmon is medium-rare to medium in temperature, about 7–8 minutes.

WHILE salmon is baking, preheat vegetable oil in deep fryer. Put sweet potato slices in fryer and fry until golden brown. Remove, drain, and keep warm for service.

TO SERVE, divide the frites in the center of two plates, and top with the king salmon fillets. Ladle the Beurre Blanc around salmon and frites and garnish with spring asparagus and chives.

*Serves 2*

*Wine Suggestion: Three Rivers White Meritage*

## For the Beurre Blanc

1   teaspoon shallots, minced
    salt & pepper to taste
¼   cup white wine

½   lemon, juice of
3   ounces unsalted butter, at room temperature

IN A saucepan, sweat shallots with salt & pepper. Add white wine and lemon juice on high heat, and reduce by three-quarters. Turn off heat, add butter and mix together. Keep warm for service.

# CIOPPINO

For best results, make the cioppino base the day before serving, adding the fresh seafood just before service.

## Ingredients

1 green pepper, seeded and julienned
1 red pepper, seeded and julienned
2 carrots, julienned
½ bunch celery, small dice
1 fennel bulb, julienned
½ red onion, julienned
½ yellow onion, julienned
4 ounces fresh garlic, coarsely chopped
  canola oil
pinch salt
1 teaspoon pepper
2 bay leaves
½ ounce dry basil leaves
¼ ounce dry thyme leaves
pinch dry tarragon leaves
pinch dry oregano leaves
½ ounce dry whole fennel seed
½ ounce granulated garlic

¼ ounce granulated onion
pinch red pepper flakes
4 ounces red wine
4 ounces white wine
2 ounces clam base (add 2 cups of water to make stock)
1 16-ounce can diced tomatoes
16 ounces ketchup
4 ounces fresh king salmon
4 ounces fresh Pacific halibut
4 ounces fresh Manila clams
4 ounces fresh Penn Cove mussels
4 ounces fresh sea scallops
4 ounces fresh large Alaskan shrimp
  Garlic Aioli (recipe follows)
  crostini, for garnish
6 chopped chives, for garnish

## Preparation

BE sure to thoroughly wash all vegetables before preparing. In a large stockpot heat on high a small amount of canola oil and sauté all vegetables until al dente. Add all dry herbs and spices. Stir to combine and sauté for 2 minutes. Deglaze pot with red wine, white wine, and clam stock stirring occasionally. Reduce by ¾ then add the diced tomatoes and ketchup. Stir in and turn heat down to medium. Let simmer for about 30 to 45 minutes. At this point, it is preferable to cool the cioppino base and store in refrigerator overnight.

WHEN ready to serve, reheat the cioppino base in a large stockpot until hot. Turn down to medium heat. Add all the fresh seafood and cook until done. Ladle cioppino into bowls and put a 1-ounce dollop of Garlic Aioli on top. Garnish with crostini and chopped chives.

*Serves 6*

*Wine Suggestion: You can match a lot of different wines with a cioppino, but a Petite Syrah would be especially nice.*

## For the Garlic Aioli

| | | | | |
|---|---|---|---|---|
| 2 | ounces fresh garlic | | ¼ | ounce fresh parsley |
| pinch | salt | | 2 | egg yolks (pasteurized) |
| pinch | pepper | | 10 | ounces canola oil |
| ½ | ounce lemon juice | | 3 | ounces half & half |
| 1 | teaspoon Dijon mustard | | | |

ADD garlic, salt, pepper, lemon juice, Dijon, parsley, and egg yolks to a food processor and combine. Leave food processor running and slowly pour in the canola oil until thick. Slowly add in enough half & half to make the aioli thin enough to pour.

# GRILLED PORK TENDERLOIN
*with Red Wine Pomegranate Demi-glace and Yukon Gold Potato "Risotto"*

## Ingredients

1  16-ounce natural pork tenderloin
½  teaspoon salt
½  tablespoon fresh ground pepper
   Yukon Gold Potato "Risotto"
     (recipe follows)

Red Wine Pomegranate Demi-glace
(recipe follows)
seasonal vegetables
fresh thyme, for garnish

## Preparation

PREHEAT a char-broiler or BBQ grill to medium-high heat. Clean all fat and silver off the pork and portion into two 8-ounce pieces. Season both sides with salt and fresh ground pepper. Cook to medium and set aside to rest for 5 minutes.

TO SERVE, place 3–4 ounces of Yukon Gold Potato "Risotto" in the center of each plate. Cut each pork tenderloin portion in half, on a bias, and place on top of the "risotto". Ladle 2–2½ ounces of the Red Wine Pomegranate Demi-glace over the pork tenderloin. Garnish with a seasonal vegetable and a sprig of fresh thyme.

### Serves 2

*Wine Suggestion:  Try a Merlot that is not too much "in your face" but more mellow.*

## For the Yukon Gold Potato "Risotto"

½  ounce canola oil
¼  cup shallots, peeled and minced
10–12  small Yukon Gold potatoes, cut in
       1-inch cubes
½  tablespoon fresh ground pepper

1  teaspoon salt
6–8  cups water
1  cup feta cheese
½  ounce fresh thyme, minced
¼  pound unsalted butter

IN A large saucepan or rondo, heat canola oil on medium heat. Add shallots and sweat off. Add the Yukon Gold potatoes, pepper, and salt and stir into the shallot until the potatoes begin to lightly brown. Add 2 cups water and continue cooking, while stirring frequently, until the potatoes absorb the water. Then add a cup at a time of the water until it is absorbed. Repeat process until potatoes are creamy and tender. Turn off heat and add feta cheese, fresh thyme, and unsalted butter to the potatoes. Incorporate until feta cheese and butter have melted. Cover and let stand for 2 minutes.

## For the Red Wine Pomegranate Demi-glace

12  ounces red wine
10  ounces pomegranate purée
½  teaspoon salt

½  tablespoon fresh ground pepper
3  tablespoons sugar
4  ounces veal demi-glace

POUR red wine and pomegranate purée into a large saucepan on high heat. Add salt, pepper, and sugar. Let reduce by half and then add the veal demi-glace. Bring to a boil, turn down to a steady roll, and reduce until sauce sticks to the back of spoon. Keep warm for service.

*Port Hadlock, south of Port Townsend on the Olympic Peninsula, was one of several important Puget Sound lumber mill towns. Lumbermen floated large rafts of logs to the mill where they were cut into lumber. Sailing ships carried the lumber to San Francisco and ports in South America, Hawaii, and Australia. Postal officials later shortened the town's name to Hadlock. ca 1900*

# Ocean Crest Resort

4651 State Route 109
Moclips, WA 98562
800-684-8439
www.oceancrestresort.com

Breakfast Daily 8:30am – 11:00am
Lunch Daily 11:00am – 2:30pm
Dinner Nightly 5:00pm – closing

# Ocean Crest Resort

### Cedar Martin, Executive Chef
### Sean Chaney, Sous Chef
### Miles Batchelder, Wine Director

The Ocean Crest Resort has offered year-round lodging for visitors to the North Washington Coast for over half a century. The resort is located on 100 acres of forested property overlooking the Pacific Ocean, offering spectacular views to its guests

Barbara Curtright Topete began with just four cabins and a bunkhouse in 1953, taking over from the previous owners. Moving with her four children to the North Beach area from Seattle, their first season began with only two units for overnight accommodations. Starting small and gradually progressing to develop the property, the Curtrights added an award-winning restaurant, cocktail lounge, health club, indoor pool, and on-site spa. Now the resort boasts 45 units, most with dramatic views of the Pacific Ocean. Some accommodations feature kitchens and wood-burning fireplaces, as well as balconies overlooking the ocean. The Curtright family still owns and operates the resort with son, Rob Curtright, acting as innkeeper. Grandson, Jess Owen, is on hand nightly to greet and serve guests in the dining room.

Over the years, the Ocean Crest restaurant has impressed a host of food and wine critics, including those from *Venture, Bon Appetit, Wine Spectator*, and *Wine Press Northwest*. The latter magazine has awarded the restaurant its *Outstanding Northwest Wine List* award since 2004, and the *Wine Spectator* has consistently given the restaurant its *Award of Excellence*. Drawing primarily from boutique wineries in the Pacific Northwest, the wine program is designed to complement and enhance the Northwest-flavored menu.

Chef Cedar Martin and Chef Sean Chaney direct a staff that is dedicated to preparing Northwest cuisine, with an emphasis on local, seasonal offerings. Delectable Pacific razor clams are collected from the resort's own beach. In the spring and early summer, the Quinault River provides fresh caught blueback salmon, and nearby Willapa Bay oysters are often on the menu. The restaurant features sustainable grass-fed, chemical-free beef raised in Oregon, as well as much locally grown organic produce. The wild mushrooms from the local forests provide a special feast of chanterelles, porcinis, and morels, as well as Oregon white truffles. All these delicacies are treated with loving care by the kitchen staff, producing succulent meals that can be enjoyed while viewing the sweeping seascape from the windows framed by wind torn spruce trees overlooking Sunset Beach.

 Award of Excellence

# Warm Spinach Salad

A signature dish of Executive Chef Cedar Martin and one of the most requested items on our dinner menu is our Warm Spinach Salad.

## Ingredients

| | |
|---|---|
| 2 tablespoons olive oil | 2 ounces brandy |
| ¼ red onion, julienned | 2 tablespoon brown sugar |
| ¼ cup mushrooms, sliced | 1 cup balsamic vinegar |
| 3 ounces pancetta, cut into cubes | ¼ cup mayonnaise |
| 6 cloves garlic, peeled | 4 cups baby spinach |
| 1 shallot, julienned | 4 strawberries, sliced |
| pinch fresh ground pepper | ¼ cup Gorgonzola cheese |

## Preparation

IN A sauté pan, sauté the red onion and mushrooms in the olive oil until tender. Set aside. Sear the pancetta in a heavy bottomed saucepan until meat is crispy and browned. Remove meat. Add garlic cloves to rendered fat and sweat until tender, about 5 minutes. Add shallot and cook until tender. Add black pepper and brown sugar, stirring until sugar is dissolved. Remove pan from heat. Add the brandy and cook off the alcohol.

RETURN pan to burner, add the balsamic vinegar and simmer until garlic is soft. Whisk in mayonnaise over heat until incorporated and thickened. Toss dressing with 4 cups of loose baby spinach. Dress the salad with strawberries and Gorgonzola cheese.

*Serves 2*

# PAN-SEARED PHEASANT

*with Chanterelle-Huckleberry Stuffing and Pan Sauce*

This dish was served at our first wine maker dinner of the 2006-2007 season (featuring Camaraderie Cellars) and was very warmly received by our guests.

## Ingredients

1   *whole pheasant*
1   *sweet onion, diced*
1   *medium carrot, diced*
1   *celery stalk, diced*
6   *parsley stems*
2   *cloves garlic*
6   *peppercorns*
    *salt & fresh ground pepper to taste*

1   *teaspoon fresh marjoram, chopped*
1   *piece of caul fat*
1   *ounce clarified butter*
1   *cup chanterelle mushrooms, cleaned & sliced*
⅛  *cup white wine*
1   *cup cream*

## Preparation

BONE pheasant thighs, leaving skin intact. Reserve bones for stock. Remove breasts, leaving skin intact.

PREHEAT oven to 350 degrees. Make a mirepoix with the diced onion, carrot, and celery. Roast bones and mirepoix in oven until a nice brown color is achieved. Place bones and roasted mirepoix in a pot and add cold water to cover. Add sachet of parley stems, 2 cloves garlic, and 6 peppercorns and add to pot. Bring pot to a light boil. Reduce heat and simmer for 1 hour. Strain contents of pot through a cheesecloth or fine mesh sieve, discarding solids and reserving stock.

PLACE pheasant thighs and breasts on a cutting board and cover with a sheet of plastic wrap. Lightly pound each piece with the back of a sauté pan to even the meat to a consistent thickness. Season to taste with salt, pepper, and chopped marjoram. Place an equal amount of Chanterelle-Huckleberry Stuffing on each piece and roll into a roulade. Cut caul fat into 4 equal squares. Wrap each roulade with a piece of the caul fat.

BRING oven back to 350 degrees. Sear each roulade in a hot pan with clarified butter until browned on both sides.  Roast in 350-degree oven until internal temperature reaches 140 degrees. Remove pheasant from the pan and let rest on clean cutting board. Strain excess fat from pan, leaving approximately 2 ounces of fat in the pan. Sauté the cup of mushrooms in fat and deglaze with white wine. Reduce by half. Add 1 cup of stock. Reduce by half. Add heavy cream. Reduce by half. Season to taste.

TO PLATE, ladle sauce on each plate. Slice each breast on the bias in half. Slice each thigh on the bias in half. Place one breast and one thigh on top of sauce on each plate.

*Makes 2 hearty servings*

*Wine Suggestion: Pinot Noir*

## For the Chanterelle-Huckleberry Stuffing

| | |
|---|---|
| 1 cup huckleberries, dried (currents may be substituted) | ½ cup chanterelle mushrooms, cleaned & sliced |
| ¼ sweet onion, julienned | ⅛ cup white wine |
| 1 clove garlic, thinly sliced | salt & pepper to taste |
| 1 ounce clarified butter | |

TO DRY the huckleberries, either use a dehydrator or dry them in a cool oven heated to 180 degrees, with the door ajar for approximately 3 hours. In a sauté pan, sweat sweet onion and garlic in clarified butter until transparent. Add mushrooms and cook until al dente. Deglaze pan with white wine. Season with salt and pepper to taste. Add dried huckleberries. Cool to room temperature.

*Sunset view at Ocean Crest Resort*

# CURRIED SEA SCALLOPS
*with Asian Slaw and Soy Lime Sauce*

## Ingredients

|  |  |
|---|---|
| 5 *fresh scallops, U10, dry-packed* | *Curry Sauce (recipe follows)* |
| *salt & pepper to taste* | *Asian Slaw (recipe follows)* |
| *clarified butter, as needed* | *Soy Lime Sauce (recipe follows)* |

## Preparation

SEASON scallops to taste with salt and pepper. Sear scallops in butter in a hot sauté pan to desired doneness. Remove scallops. Heat Curry Sauce in the same pan to release fond.
TO SERVE, drizzle warm Curry Sauce around edge of plate. Place scallops along edge of plate over the sauce. Toss Asian Slaw with Soy Lime Sauce and place in the middle of the plate. Serve with jasmine rice.

*Serves 2*

## For the Curry Sauce

|  |  |
|---|---|
| 1 *tablespoon curry powder* | ¼ *cup Manzanilla sherry* |
| 2 *tablespoons clarified butter* | 1 *cup heavy cream* |
| 1 *tablespoon garlic, chopped* | 4 *13.5-ounce cans coconut milk* |

TOAST the curry powder in a heavy-bottomed brazier until aromatic. Add butter and garlic, allowing garlic to sweat. Add sherry and allow alcohol to burn off. Add heavy cream and coconut milk. Bring mixture to a simmer and reduce by half.

## For the Asian Slaw

|  |  |
|---|---|
| 1 *cup green cabbage, finely shredded* | ½ *red pepper, finely diced* |
| ¼ *cup red cabbage, finely shredded* | ½ *sweet onion, finely julienned* |
| 1 *medium carrot, peeled and finely julienned* |  |

MIX ingredients together in a small bowl and set aside.

## For the Soy Lime Sauce

|  |  |
|---|---|
| 1 *cup soy sauce* | ¼ *cup brown sugar* |
| 1 *cup teriyaki sauce* | 2 *limes, halved* |

PLACE soy sauce, teriyaki sauce, and brown sugar in a small saucepan, and squeeze lime halves over mixture. Add squeezed limes to mixture and bring ingredients to a simmer and let cook until sugar is dissolved. Cool in refrigerator. Discard lime halves before serving.

# The Depot

## The DEPOT Restaurant

1208 38th Place & L
Seaview, WA
360-642-7880
www.depotrestaurantdining.com

Summer Months:
Tuesday – Sunday from 5:00pm
"School" Months:
Wednesday – Sunday from 5:00pm

# The Depot Restaurant

### *Michael Lalewicz, Executive Chef/Proprietor*
### *Nancy Gorshe, Manager/Proprietor*

Coastal visitors and locals alike have been drawn to the hundred-year-old train depot in Seaview to enjoy the superbly prepared cuisine created by Western Culinary Institute graduate Michael Lalewicz. Both Seaview and The Depot have interesting histories. The area became popular as a vacation site as early as the 1870s, when families arrived to camp in the Willows, north of Cape Disappointment. As the area grew, a railroad was built to replace the old stage line that carried goods from the Ilwaco wharf, just south of Sea View to Oysterville. Many of the goods had come across the Columbia River on steamers from Portland and Astoria, Oregon. However, the ships could only reach the Ilwaco wharf when the tide was in mid-flood, causing the train departures to vary. It is likely that the Ilwaco line was the only organized railroad to operate by a tide table, hence its nickname, the "Clamshell Railroad."

Frank Strauhal, a summer camper at the Willows, purchased the store and bathhouse in Seaview, and offered the railroad a lot, if a depot was erected on his site, therefore increasing the traffic to his properties. A wooden platform shed was built as a train stop on the current Seaview Depot site. In 1900, the railroad ownership changed hands, and in 1905 a directors' meeting authorized the construction of a regular depot to replace the platform shed in Seaview. That building is the one that has become home to Michael Lalewicz's and Nancy Gorshe's restaurant.

The wide variety of flavors on The Depot Restaurant's menu is the creation of a chef with an extensive exposure to ethnic foods. Chef Michael's cooking roots germinate from suburban Detroit, where his youth was filled with the sights, tastes, and scents of Polish, German, Jewish, Greek, and Italian foods. The rich bounty of wild game in the Midwest gave Michael a chance to learn the techniques of cooking wild game, and grandmothers who emigrated from the Deep South taught him southern and soul food recipes. In the 1980s, Michael lived between Washington D.C. and the Chesapeake Bay, where he mastered seafood recipes and the products of southern Maryland and Virginia. He also traveled extensively to the great food cities and regions of the world. While in Portland, Oregon Michael served as Sous Chef at Restaurant Toulouse and he developed and opened the Greek kitchen of Portland's premier jazz club, Jimmy Mak's. Now, as owner of The Depot Restaurant, he is able to create gastronomic delights for guests in a quaint and casual setting.

# GARLIC CRAB MAC

Chef Michael Lalewicz put this recipe on as a "comfort food" special for one season's menu. Now customers won't let us take it off the menu!

## Ingredients

- 2 cups cavatappi or elbow pasta noodles
- 2 tablespoons fresh garlic, chopped
- 1 teaspoon black pepper
- 2 tablespoons light olive oil (not extra virgin)
- 2 tablespoons unsalted butter
- 1 tablespoons fresh squeezed lemon juice
- ½ cup white wine

- 3 cups heavy cream
- 5 ounces fresh Dungeness crab
- 4 ounces provolone cheese, shredded
- 2 tablespoons Parmesan Reggiano, grated
- 3 tablespoons panko breadcrumbs, toasted
- 1 tablespoon Italian parsley, chopped

## Preparation

BOIL good quality pasta for about 3–5 minutes. Do not rinse pasta.

AT the same time, place fresh chopped garlic, black pepper, olive oil, and unsalted butter in large sauté pan on high heat. Cook until butter is melted. Add fresh squeezed lemon juice and white wine to mixture and reduce until liquid is nearly gone. Add heavy cream and the cooked drained pasta while still hot. Bring cream and pasta mixture to a boil and reduce heat. Then add fresh Dungeness crab and shredded provolone cheese. Simmer for 2 minutes.

POUR into large bowl to serve. Sprinkle with grated Parmesan Reggiano cheese, then toasted panko breadcrumbs, and top with chopped parsley.

### Serves 2 as an entrée or 4 as an appetizer

*Wine Suggestion: With this rich dish, enjoy a light medium-bodied white wine such as a Fumé Blanc by Barnard Griffin, Washington*

# OYSTER GRATIN

The Depot Restaurant's location between the mouth of the Columbia River and the Willapa Bay, one of the nation's largest and most pristine estuaries, allows Chef Michael to pick up fresh Willapa Oysters each day on his way to the kitchen.

## Ingredients

5  tablespoons unsalted butter, approximately
1½  cups all-purpose flour, divided
½  teaspoon salt & pepper
8  medium oysters, shucked
3  russet potatoes, washed but not peeled
4  fresh whole garlic cloves, minced

3  cups heavy cream
4  ramekins (see instructions below)
   Porcini Mushroom Cream Sauce
   (recipe follows)
   edible fresh flowers and herbs, for garnish

## Preparation

THE ramekins need to be at least 4–5 inches deep and 3–4 inches across. Small restaurant style soup cups work best. The butter must be at room temperature to ease spreading into the ramekins. After evenly coating the inside of each ramekin with a tablespoon of butter, drop a tablespoon of flour into them and shake to evenly coat the inside with flour. Shake off excess flour into mixing bowl. Place the rest of flour into mixing bowl and season with salt and pepper. Place oysters into flour mixture and evenly coat them. Slice potatoes paper-thin, do not rinse potatoes after slicing them and always use starchy potatoes such as russets.

PREHEAT oven to 400 degrees. Place a teaspoon of softened butter in bottom of each ramekin, then layer slices of potato in bottom of ramekins alternating layers with salt and pepper. When ramekins are less than half full, put in 2 oysters that have been tossed in seasoned flour and add fresh minced garlic. Finish layering with rest of potatoes until the ramekins are full. Fill with heavy cream; wait a few seconds until the cream settles, then top with more cream. Place ramekins on a sheet pan that has 1- to 2-inch sides and put in oven for 45 minutes to 1 hour.

WHEN the cream is bubbling and the top is golden brown, this is an indication that the gratin is ready to come out of the oven. Often times the top of the gratin will look very dark. This is normal because some ovens vary in temperature and run a little hotter than others. Remove the sheet pan from the oven and let rest a few minutes. With an oven mitt hold the hot ramekin, running a paring knife around the inside edge of the ramekin, freeing the crispy bits of cream and potato from the sides. Place the ramekins upside down on a hot sheet pan and let sit a few minutes or hold until serving.

WHEN ready to serve lift gratin and ramekin with flat metal spatula onto plate. Remove ramekin and spoon Porcini Mushroom Cream Sauce around the gratin and garnish with editable flowers and fresh herbs.

*Yields: 4 entrées, perfect for brunch.*

*Wine Suggestion: Accompany with a fresh crisp Spanish Cava by Segura Vidas*

## For the Porcini Mushroom Cream Sauce

| | |
|---|---|
| 1 cup dry porcini mushrooms | 1 tablespoon sherry vinegar |
| 2 cups boiling water | 1 tablespoon fresh thyme, finely chopped |
| 2 tablespoons unsalted butter | 2 cups heavy cream |
| 1 shallot, finely chopped | ½ teaspoon kosher salt |
| 2 fresh garlic cloves, finely chopped | ½ teaspoon cracked white pepper |

ADD boiling water to dry porcini mushrooms and hold, covered, for 15 minutes. Squeeze water out of mushrooms and chop mushrooms coarsely. Retain the water.

IN A sauté pan, on medium heat, add butter, finely chopped shallots and garlic, cook until opaque. Add sherry vinegar and cook until all liquid is reduced. Add fresh thyme and cook for 1 minute. Add porcini mushrooms and all remaining mushroom liquid to the pan. Reduce until small amount of liquid is visible at the bottom of the pan. Add cream and bring to simmer. Add salt and pepper.

NOTE: If using fresh porcini mushrooms, chop them fine and pan sear at high heat with oil and butter until brown. Add mushrooms to the sauce last, then simmer for a few minutes so the mushrooms can exude flavor into sauce.

# THAI PEANUT CALAMARI

A delicious combination that is the most popular appetizer on The Depot's menu.

## Ingredients

1 bunch green onions, chopped, divided
¼ cup whole fresh garlic cloves
1 cup salted toasted peanuts, chopped, divided
¾ cup rice wine vinegar
½ bunch cilantro
¼ cup toasted sesame oil
¼ cup Asian fish sauce
½ fresh habanero pepper
1 cup light olive oil (not extra virgin)

5 won ton wrapper sheets
6 cups vegetable oil for deep frying
4 cups rice flour
pinch cayenne pepper
1 tablespoon granulated garlic
4 tablespoons cornstarch
6 ounces calamari tubes and tentacles, cut in bite-size pieces
fresh spinach

## Preparation

PLACE in blender ½ of the bunch of green onions, the garlic, ½ cup of the salted peanuts, the rice wine vinegar, cilantro, sesame oil, fish sauce, and habanero pepper. Place lid on blender and turn on low. As soon as all ingredients are combined, and while blender is still on, remove lid and add the olive oil until emulsified; less than 1 minute.

PREHEAT deep fat fryer to 350 degrees. Cut the won ton wrappers into small strips. Deep fry until golden brown and reserve them for final assembly.

COMBINE rice flour, cayenne pepper, garlic powder, and cornstarch in a bowl and mix well. Toss the calamari pieces in the rice flour mixture and shake off excess flour in wire mesh colander. Place in 350-degree deep fat fryer until calamari floats. Drain calamari. Place in bowl with fried won ton skins and 4–5 tablespoons of sauce. Toss until well coated. Serve on plate over a handful of fresh spinach. Top with remaining green onions and chopped peanuts. Serve remaining sauce on the side.

### Serves 4 as an appetizer

*Beverage Suggestions: Accompany this dish with a spicy Shiraz such as Jacob's Creek Reserve or a Pilsner Urquell, Czechoslovakia*

# OLD BAY DUNGENESS CRAB-STUFFED SOLE

Depot owners Chef Michael and wife Nancy met in Maryland. They loved Blue Crab and Baltimore's Old Bay Seasoning®. They cherish Dungeness Crab!

## Ingredients

½  cup red bell pepper, chopped
½  cup medium onion, chopped
2  cloves garlic, chopped
2  stalks celery, chopped
2  tablespoons butter
½  cup white wine
2  tablespoons Old Bay Seasoning®, divided
4  ounces cream cheese

½  cup Parmesan cheese, grated
2  cups cooked Dungeness crabmeat
½  cup cream
¼  cup panko breadcrumbs
2  6-ounce sole fillets
2  cups all-purpose flour
4  tablespoons olive oil
4  green onions, chopped

## Preparation

PREHEAT oven to 500 degrees. Sauté bell pepper, onion, garlic, and celery in butter and wine until liquid has evaporated. Add 1 tablespoon of Old Bay Seasoning®. While hot, add cream cheese, grated Parmesan cheese, and the cooked Dungeness crabmeat. When ingredients are well combined, remove one quarter of this mixture and place in separate saucepan, add the cream and heat. This will be the sauce.

TO the remaining three quarters of the mixture add the panko breadcrumbs and let cool. This is the stuffing for the fish.

FILL sole fillets with the stuffing and roll them up. Mix all-purpose flour and the remaining tablespoon Old Bay Seasoning®. Heat a sauté pan with the olive oil. Dredge the rolled fillets in the flour mixture and place seam-side down in the hot sauté pan. Sear the fillets on both sides, about 1 minute on each side. Place pan in 500-degree oven to bake for 5 minutes.
To serve, place stuffed sole on plates and pour sauce over the baked fish. Top with chopped green onions. This is lovely served with hazelnut cranberry wild rice pilaf and sautéed broccolini.

*Serves 2 as an entrée.*

*Wine Suggestions: A smooth Semillon such as a Beresan or Bergevin Lane Vineyards from Walla Walla would be a perfect match for this dish.*

*Denny family picnic on Snoqualmie River. In the 1890's and the first several decades of the 1900's, members of the Denny family spent a good deal of time in the Cascade Mountains, where they mined for gold and enjoyed the outdoors. Photo taken in 1917 or 1918.*

# Waterstreet Café

610 Water Street SE
Olympia, WA 98501
360-709-9090
www.waterstreetcafeandbar.com

Monday through Thursday
11:30am – 9:00pm
Friday 11:30am – 10:30pm
Saturday 4:30pm – 10:30pm
Sunday 4:30pm – 9:00pm

# Waterstreet Café

*Jeff Taylor, Proprietor*
*Leonard Young, Director of Wine Operations*

The South Puget Sound area of Washington has been inhabited for at least 11,000 years; first by the Southern Coast Salish Indians. The area was originally called "Chithoot"—meaning "bear"—as it attracted hungry bears that grubbed for the tasty skunk cabbage that grew in the swampy ground. The Indians found the area rich in foods, from the juicy berries, to the plentiful game, to the oysters, clams, and salmon found in the coves and rivers feeding into the sound. It wasn't until the 1840s that white men settled in the region and started designing a town in 1850. In 1889, Washington became a state, but Olympia was not chosen as the first state capital. The capital was sited in many cities—Vancouver, Steilacoom, Seattle, Tacoma, and Port Townsend—before finally being placed in Olympia.

The Waterstreet Café and Bar in downtown Olympia is located near the capital building. The restaurant is located in the historic American Legion building that is on the National Register of Historic Places. The main dining room and open-air patio offer views of Capital Lake, Heritage Park, and the Capital Building.

The cuisine is best described as contemporary American and is beautifully presented, using the highest quality ingredients. The menu features many mouthwatering delights. For appetizers, guests can enjoy Pork Empanadas, a concoction of succulent Carlton Farms pork and sweet potato filled pastry with blackened garbanzo bean chutney, roasted poblano crema, and smoked paprika oil. Roasted Crab & Piquillo Pepper Gratin is another favorite, and a special artisan cheese plate offers gourmet cheeses from around the world. Fresh salads and soups are plentiful as well as unique pizzas and pasta dishes. Vegetable lovers can choose from such delectable entrées as Portobello Wellington, a grilled portobello with porcini-hazelnut pâté in a gruyere-filled puff pastry with a black olive cabernet sauce. Other entrées on a recent menu include Coconut Crusted Snapper and Rustic Italian Meatloaf. Outstanding desserts are also offered, such as Whiskey Pecan Chocolate Torte and Grand Marnier Blood Orange Crème Brûlée.

The pièce de résistance at Waterstreet Café, however, is their superb wine cellar and wine service. The wines are maintained with careful temperature control and are served in beautiful Riedel stemware. About a third of the collection is from the fine vineyards of Washington. The balance of the list spans the globe and is selected on two main criteria: They must be delicious in their own right and must be harmonious companions to Waterstreet's fine cuisine. This attention to detail has earned the café the *Award of Excellence* from *Wine Spectator* for 2006 and 2007.

 Award of Excellence

# LOBSTER CHOWDER WITH PARMESAN CRISPS

This is a luxurious soup that is a meal in itself, probably the most popular and requested soup we have served at the restaurant.

## Ingredients

| | |
|---|---|
| 1½ quarts heavy cream | ⅔ cup chicken stock |
| 3 tablespoons olive oil | 2 tablespoons tomato purée |
| 2 cups onion, diced | ⅓ cup parsley, chopped |
| 1 cup celery, diced | ⅓ cup flour |
| ¾ cup carrot, diced | 2 tablespoons green Tabasco® |
| 4 ounces sherry | 1 tablespoon dried oregano |
| 1 quart Yukon Gold potatoes, peeled & diced | 1 tablespoon dried thyme |
| | ½ pound cooked or raw lobster meat |
| 16 ounces clam juice | Parmesan Crisps (recipe follows) |

## Preparation

SIMMER heavy cream in a 2-quart saucepan until its volume is reduced by half. Be careful not to boil. When reduced by half, set aside.

IN AN 8-quart heavy-bottomed saucepan, heat olive oil over medium heat and add onion, celery, and carrot. Cook vegetables until onions and celery are translucent. Deglaze with sherry. Add potatoes, clam juice, and chicken stock to vegetable mixture. Simmer until potatoes are firm but cooked through. Add all other ingredients to vegetable mixture and simmer for about 10 minutes, to incorporate herbs and flour. Add reduced heavy cream and simmer for another 10 minutes. Season with salt and pepper to taste.

TO SERVE, pour chowder in bowls, place bowls on plates with 2 or 3 Parmesan Crisps on the side.

### Serves 8–10

*Wine Suggestion: Forgeron Chardonnay, Columbia Valley 2005 (Washington) or La Soufrandière Pouilly Vinzelles "Les Quarts" 2003 (France)*

## For the Parmesan Crisps

2 cups grated Parmigiano Reggiano

PREHEAT oven to 350 degrees. Line a lightly greased baking sheet with parchment paper. Spoon level tablespoons of cheese onto sheet, four inches apart. Pat mounds into 3½-inch long ovals of even thickness. Bake on middle rack for 4–5 minutes, until golden in color and lacy in appearance. Cool completely on baking sheet.

# ROASTED BEET & SEARED BUTTERLEAF SALAD
## *with Shallot Vinaigrette*

This salad greatly benefits from organic vegetables—use them if possible! The idea of grilling or searing lettuce may be odd but, if done properly, it can enhance any salad.

## Ingredients

1 tablespoon butter
1 cup walnuts, chopped
½ cup sugar
¼ cup water
1 pound golden or red beets, trimmed & quartered
2 medium carrots, julienned

¼ cup extra virgin olive oil, divided
salt & pepper
1 large head butter leaf lettuce, rinsed & quartered
1 cup Stilton, crumbles (or other high-quality blue cheese)

## Preparation

PREHEAT oven to 300 degrees. Butter a large baking pan. Combine nuts, sugar, and water in a heavy saucepan over medium heat. Cook, stirring, until walnuts are coated with a thick syrup, about 15 minutes. Spread walnuts in baking pan, sprinkle with salt, and bake for 15 minutes. Turn with a spatula and bake for another 15 minutes. Remove from oven and let cool.

RAISE oven temperature to 450 degrees. Toss beets in some of the olive oil and sprinkle with salt and pepper. Lay quartered beets on a sheet pan, cover loosely with foil, and roast in oven for 1–1½ hours, or until tender. Remove beets from oven and immerse them in ice water for 5 minutes. Remove beets from ice water and peel off skins. Cut beets into ½-inch dice and set aside.

HEAT a cast iron skillet over medium heat. Coat lettuce quarters with remaining olive oil, and sprinkle with salt and pepper. Working in batches of 2 quarters at a time, lightly sear lettuce quarters in skillet for 1–2 minutes on each flat side. Do not overcook or burn—lettuce should remain crisp! Remove lettuce from skillet and set aside, keeping warm.

WHEN ready to serve, rough chop warm lettuce quarters. In a large salad bowl, combine chopped lettuce, diced beets, julienne carrots, candied walnuts, and crumbled Stilton. Add Shallot Vinaigrette to taste and lightly toss. Finish with salt and pepper to taste and serve.

### *Serves 4*

*Wine Suggestions: Domaine de Bellivière Côteaux du Loir "Le Rouge Gorge" 2003, France, or K Walla Walla Valley "The Boy" 2004, Washington*

## For the Shallot Vinaigrette

2 ounces shallots
¼ cup parsley, chopped
1 tablespoon sugar
½ cup rice wine vinegar

1¼ cup canola oil
1 teaspoon water, as needed
salt & ground black pepper to taste

USING a food processor, purée the shallots. Add parsley, sugar, and vinegar. Slowly add canola oil, until fully emulsified. Adjust texture with water—it should not be too thick or too thin. Finish with salt and pepper to taste. This can be made a day in advance, and will keep for up to 3 days.

*Two women pack apples in crates at an unidentified orchard in central Washington. The women wear long skirts, aprons, blouses with full sleeves and hats. September 1906*

# PROSCIUTTO-WRAPPED SALMON
## *with Fall Vegetable Hash and Toasted Mustard Seed Vinaigrette*

This is one of our wine steward's favorite dishes because it pairs so beautifully with pure, terroir-driven Pinot Noir.

## Ingredients

4   7-ounce skinless wild salmon or steelhead filets
    olive oil
    salt & ground black pepper to taste
4   large fresh sage leaves
4   thin, 8- by 3-inch slices prosciutto de Parma

    canola oil
2   tablespoons white wine
    Fall Vegetable Hash (recipe follows)
¼   cup Parmigiano Reggiano, grated
    Toasted Mustard Seed Vinaigrette (recipe follows)
2   ounces baby arugula, for garnish

## Preparation

RUB salmon filets with olive oil, salt, and pepper. Place a sage leaf on middle of each filet and wrap with a slice of prosciutto. Heat a large, heavy sauté pan over high heat, until smoking. Coat entire pan with a thin film of canola oil. Working in batches, 2 salmon filets at a time, gently add prosciutto-wrapped filets into pan, gently shaking pan to prevent prosciutto from sticking. Sear filets for 4–5 minutes on one side, turn over, and sear for 2 more minutes, for medium rare. Repeat with second pair of filets. Remove filets from pan, set aside, and keep warm.

POUR off any excess oil and deglaze pan by whisking in the white wine. Add Fall Vegetable Hash to pan, and then add Parmesan and herbs. Lightly toss, and drizzle with olive oil.

TO SERVE, divide hash equally among 4 plates. Rest salmon filets on hash and lightly drizzle Toasted Mustard Seed Vinaigrette over all. Garnish with the baby arugula.

### *Serves 4*

*Wine Suggestions: Evesham Wood Pinot Noir Willamette Valley "Le Puits Sec" 2004, Oregon or Sylvie Esmonin Gevrey-Chambertin, France*

## For the Fall Vegetable Hash

½   pound fingerling potatoes (organic, if available)
½   cup olive oil, divided
    salt & ground black pepper to taste
2   tablespoons unsalted butter
1   pound wild mushrooms, cleaned and torn into big pieces by hand

1   tablespoon shallot, minced
1   tablespoon garlic, minced
½   pound Brussels sprouts, chopped
1   cup chicken stock
1   teaspoon fresh sage, chopped
1   teaspoon fresh thyme, chopped

PREHEAT oven to 450 degrees. Halve fingerling potatoes, toss in some of the olive oil and add salt and pepper to taste. Spread potatoes on a large baking sheet and roast in oven for 45 minutes, turning every 15 minutes. Potatoes should be firm, do not overcook! Remove potatoes from oven and cool. Dice into ¼-inch cubes.

HEAT a large cast iron skillet over medium-high heat. Melt butter in skillet and add 2 table-spoons olive oil and the mushrooms. Sprinkle with salt and sauté for 5 minutes, until water has been released from mushrooms and has evaporated. Add shallots, garlic, cubed potatoes, Brussels sprouts, and salt & pepper to taste. Sauté for 5 minutes, and then add chicken stock. Sauté for 5 more minutes and put in oven for 10 minutes, turning mixture over after the first 5 minutes. Remove from oven and sprinkle with sage and thyme, and keep warm for service.

## For the Toasted Mustard Seed Vinaigrette

| | |
|---|---|
| ¼  cup mustard seeds | 1  tablespoon sugar |
| 1  tablespoon shallot, minced | ¼  cider vinegar |
| 1  teaspoon parsley, chopped | ½  cup grape seed oil |
| 1  tablespoon Dijon mustard | ¼  cup extra virgin olive oil |
| 1  tablespoon yellow mustard | salt & pepper to taste |

OVER low heat in a medium saucepan, toast mustard seeds for 8 minutes. Place toasted seeds, shallot, parsley, mustards, sugar, and vinegar into a mixing bowl. Gently whisk the ingredients together. While continuing to whisk, slowly incorporate grape seed oil, and then the olive oil. Finish with salt and pepper.

# OREGON LAMB SHANK
*with Cedar Roasted Mushrooms, Roasted Pistachio Citrus Gremolata, and Mascarpone Thyme Whipped Polenta*

## Ingredients

| | |
|---|---|
| 1 cup canola oil | 3 bay leaves |
| 4 12-ounce lamb fore shanks | 2 tablespoons whole black peppercorns |
| 2 cups flour | 4 sprigs thyme |
| 1 tablespoon salt | 4 sprigs rosemary |
| 1 tablespoon freshly ground black pepper | Mascarpone Whipped Polenta (recipe follows) |
| 2 cups onions, diced | 1 tablespoon extra virgin olive oil |
| 1 cup celery, diced | Cedar Roasted Mushrooms (recipe follows) |
| 1 cup carrot, diced | Roasted Pistachio Citrus Gremolata (recipe follows) |
| 2 tablespoons tomato paste | thyme sprigs, for garnish |
| 1 750ml bottle red wine | |
| 1 quart chicken stock | |
| 4 cloves garlic | |

## Preparation

PREHEAT oven to 250 degrees. Place ½ cup of canola in a large, 6-inch deep, heavy pan over medium-high heat until just smoking. Combine flour with salt and pepper. Dredge lamb shanks in seasoned flour, shaking off excess flour. Working in batches of 2 shanks at a time, gently place lamb in pan and brown on all sides, being careful not to burn flour. When browned, set shanks aside to rest and repeat with remaining shanks and rest of canola oil. Pour off and discard excess oil.

ADD vegetables and tomato paste to pan and sauté for 8 minutes. Deglaze pan with 1 cup of the wine, whisk, and simmer for 5 minutes. Add chicken stock, garlic, bay leaves, peppercorns, thyme, rosemary, and remaining wine. Bring to a simmer and add shanks along with salt and pepper to taste.

COVER pan with aluminum foil and place in 205-degree oven. Bake for 2½–3 hours, or until meat is just falling off the bone. Remove from oven, remove shanks from pan and set them aside to rest. Reduce cooking liquid by two-thirds, then strain and return to pan. Add lamb shanks and keep warm until polenta and mushrooms are prepared.

TO SERVE, divide Mascarpone Whipped Polenta among 4 plates, placing in center of each plate. Top polenta with a lamb shank. Whisk extra virgin olive oil into lamb sauce and pour sauce over shank and polenta. Top each shank with Roasted Pistachio Citrus Gremolata and Cedar Roasted Mushrooms, and garnish with a thyme sprig.

*Serves 4*

*Wine Suggestions: Abbona Barolo "Pressenda" 2000, Italy or Cadence Red Mountain "Bel Canto" 2004, Washington*

## For the Mascarpone Whipped Polenta

6 cups water
2 cups heavy cream
2 cups instant polenta
3 tablespoons mascarpone

1 tablespoon fresh thyme leaves
1 tablespoon coarse salt, or to taste
⅛ cup Parmesan cheese, grated

BRING water to boil, add cream and bring back to a simmer. Slowly add polenta, stirring continually for about 30 minutes, until texture is similar to mashed potatoes. Stir in mascarpone, thyme, salt, and Parmesan. Keep warm for service.

## For the Roasted Pistachio Citrus Gremolata

1 cup shelled pistachios
1 tablespoon shallot, chopped
1 tablespoon lemon zest
1 tablespoon orange zest
½ cup parsley, chopped
¼ cup mint, chopped

¼ cup chives, chopped
3 tablespoons extra virgin olive oil
2 tablespoons fresh orange juice
½ tablespoon orange brandy
salt & ground black pepper to taste

TOAST pistachios for 10 minutes over low heat, shaking pan periodically. Remove pistachios from pan and place in food processor with all other ingredients except salt and pepper. Pulse 7 times, until texture is coarse—do not over blend! Add salt and pepper to taste. This gremolata can be made a day in advance, and will keep for 3 days.

## For the Cedar Roasted Mushrooms

1 pound cleaned mushrooms
   (chanterelle, porcini, portobello, or
   shiitake)
1 tablespoon extra virgin olive oil

2 sprigs thyme
   salt & ground black pepper to taste
1 6-inch by 10-inch cedar plank

PREHEAT oven to 400 degrees. Toss mushrooms with olive oil, thyme, salt, and pepper. Spread evenly on cedar plank. Roast in oven until barely done and water has evaporated out of mushrooms, about 10–15 minutes. Remove from oven, cover mushrooms with foil, and keep warm for service.

U.S.S DECATUR

*During the early 1850s, hostility grew between the native peoples and the new settlers in the Puget Sound region. The "Decatur" and several other government ships were moved to the area to protect the settlers. On January 26, 1856, following word of a planned attack on Seattle, troops on the "Decatur" fired howitzers into the forest beyond Third Avenue where a group of angry Native Americans had gathered. The Indians retreated, burning buildings as they went. [not before 1902]*

# Brix 25°

7707 Pioneer Way
Gig Harbor, WA 98335
253-858-6626
www.harborbrix.com

Dinner Sunday – Thursday
4:30pm – 9:30pm
Dinner Friday & Saturday
4:30pm – 11:00pm

# Brix 25°

*Nick & Joleen Reynolds, Proprietors*
*Jason Winniford, General Manager*
*Daniel Hutchinson, Executive Chef*
*Leia Reiser, Pastry Chef*
*Bret Schnorenberg, Sommelier*

Nestled in the south end of Puget Sound is the quiet waterfront village of Gig Harbor. The Gig Harbor Peninsula area offers a spectacular view of Mt. Rainier that has graced the pages of many calendars and tour books around the world. It is a perfect place to relax, refresh, and rejuvenate.

If fine dining and fine wines are a favorite form of relaxation, Brix 25° is perfect for you. Located in historic downtown Gig Harbor, the restaurant is situated in a freestanding building on Pioneer Way. Considered historic by Gig Harbor standards, the building was constructed in 1952 and originally called Don's Drugs, the village's first pharmacy and drug store. Later, it became Marcos Italian Ristorante and, in the summer of 2004, the building was revamped and remodeled as Brix 25° by Mark and Jill Wambold. In April 2006, Nick and Joleen Reynolds purchased the building and restaurant.

Executive Chef Dan Hutchinson and his talented staff strive for perfection with every plate, and each dish is treated with care and attention. As Chef Dan says, "We want every guest to feel the love we put into our food." This dedication has reaped rewards. The City of Gig Harbor voted the restaurant the award of *Best Fine Dining in 2006*.

The wine program at Brix 25° is an ongoing labor of love also. In fact the name of the restaurant is taken from the term that was originated in the 19th century by Adolf Brix, who discovered the technique of passing light through a solution to determine the concentration of the solution by the angle or degree by which the light was refracted. This discovery led to the Brix scale as a unit of measure indicating the concentration of sugar in fruit juice, which is used widely in the production of wines. The restaurant's wine program currently offers over 200 selections, and is dedicated to serving wines exclusively from the Northwest. Elegant Riedel crystal is used as the standard stemware in the restaurant. In 2006, Brix 25° received the *Washington Wine Grand Award* from the Washington Wine Commission, and also received the *Award of Excellence* from *Wine Spectator* magazine.

 Award of Excellence

# Martini Salad with Pepper Jelly Vinaigrette

This salad works almost equally well as a dessert or palette-cleansing course as it does at the beginning of a meal, because of its sweet and refreshing flavor profile. It is a menu adaptation of a salad created for a winemaker's diner we did. The dressing was inspired by a batch of homemade pepper jelly that our owner's wife made for all the employees as Christmas gifts. There was a great deal left over and, in the mind of not letting it go to waste, our pastry/pantry chef, Leia, created this fantastic dressing.

## Ingredients

- 1 honeydew melon, balled or cubed
- 1 cantaloupe melon, balled or cubed
- 1 large pear, sliced thin
- 1 English cucumber, sliced thin on the bias, 3-inch slices
- 12 thin slices of prosciutto, julienne stripped
- 1 bunch cilantro, stems removed
- 1 pint cherry tomatoes, halved
- Pepper Jelly Vinaigrette (recipe follows)
- ¾ pound baby spinach
- fresh mint sprig and berries, for garnish

## Preparation

COMBINE all ingredients in a large mixing bowl and place over a bed of spinach and garnish with fresh mint sprig and fresh berries. We serve this salad in a stemless martini glass (hence the name) but any service ware is fine. If you can find the glasses, they certainly make for a striking presentation.

*Serves 4–6*

*Suggested Wine: 2005 Van Duzer Pinot Gris, Willamette Valley*

## For the Pepper Jelly Vinaigrette

- 8 ounces sweet pepper jelly (your favorite brand from the store is fine and you can mix it up with spicy jelly as well)
- 1 bunch fresh cilantro whole, stem and all
- 2 garlic cloves
- ½ teaspoon salt
- ½ teaspoon black pepper
- 2 cups champagne vinegar or white balsamic vinegar
- 2 cups extra virgin olive oil

ADD all ingredients except olive oil to a large food processor and blend, scraping the sides of the bowl. On highest speed, slowly drizzle oil into mixture to thicken and emulsify. Refrigerate. This dressing can be made ahead and will keep for a month if tightly sealed. It's great on mixed greens or even as a light sauce for grilled fish.

# FILET MIGNON
### *with Caramelized Cipollini Onions and Smoked Bacon*

This steak is full of rich flavors with the bacon and the cipollini onions, porcini mushrooms, and Madeira. The sauce is the result of a weekend barbecue at one of our line cook's homes. He came back to work on Tuesday and made the sauce for us and it was clear that it had to be that night's special. Now we put it on everything from steak and pork chops to scallops, and even duck. We serve it on Yukon Gold mashed potatoes with white pepper, but your favorite mashed potato recipe would work just fine; even mashed sweet potatoes to add a little fall charm to the meal.

## Ingredients

 4 8-ounce beef tenderloin filets
   salt and pepper to taste
   olive oil spray
16 pieces asparagus

Cippolini Onion Sauce (recipe follows)
*your favorite mashed potatoes*
*rosemary sprigs for garnish*

## Preparation

PREHEAT grill and spray with olive oil spray. Season each steak heavily with salt and pepper and then spray steaks with olive oil. Grill covered, making a ¼ turn then flipping and another ¼ turn throughout cooking time, to give the meat diamond grill marks. Grill asparagus and season with salt and pepper.

ASSEMBLE by stacking the asparagus on top of the mashed potatoes and the steaks on top of that. Top the tower with the Cipollini Onion Sauce and garnish with a rosemary sprig.

*Serves 4*

*Suggested wine: 2003 Patit Creek Cellars Cabernet Sauvignon, Walla Walla Valley*

## For Cippolini Onion Sauce

12 cipollini onions, roasted and skins
   removed
36 bacon lardons
 3 ounces porcini mushrooms
 ½ ounce fresh rosemary, chopped
 ½ ounce fresh oregano, chopped
 2 cups Madeira

½ cup veal demi-glace (can substitute
   double strength beef stock if
   necessary, but use low sodium variety
   and watch salt level)
 2 tablespoons unsalted Plugrá butter, or
   unsalted sweet butter

ADD bacon to a medium sauté pan and render fat. Add onions and mushrooms and sauté for 1 minute. Deglaze with Madeira and reduce till almost dry. Add demi-glace and reduce by half. Finish with herbs and whisk in butter to bring the sauce to nappe.

# WEATHERVANE SCALLOPS
*with Strawberry Lime Reduction and Mixed Greens with Candied Nuts and Dried Fruit*

I serve this dish as a chef's appetizer upon request, depending on availability of the weathervane scallops, which truly make the dish. The tangy sweet sauce pairs very well with a sweet white wine and makes for a refreshing course for an afternoon get together or as a lighter course between two meat courses. You can use any kind of candied nut, but I prefer to dust mine with a touch of cayenne to accentuate the sweetness of the overall flavor profile. The quantities can also be increased to serve as a light lunch or main course.

## Ingredients

4   large (U-10) weathervane scallops
2   tablespoons pure olive oil
3   tablespoons chicken stock
½   cup baby mixed greens
2   ounces candied walnuts, or other candied nut

2   ounces sun-dried blueberries
    Strawberry Lime Reduction
4   slices of English cucumber (rounds), ⅛-inch thick
    fresh herbs or edible flowers for garnish

## Preparation

PREHEAT oven to 400 degrees. Heat olive oil in a small sauté pan and sear scallops in oil until caramelized. Flip scallops and add chicken stock. Finish scallops in oven for 2 minutes.

ARRANGE greens in center of a plate and place cucumber rounds on plate at 12, 3, 6, and 9 o'clock. Sprinkle nuts and berries over plate and place scallops on cucumber rounds. Drizzle salad and scallops with Strawberry Lime Reduction and garnish with fresh herbs or edible flowers.

*Serves 4 as an appetizer*

*Wine Suggestion: 2005 Brooks Amycas white table wine, Oregon*

## For the Strawberry Lime Reduction

2   tablespoons puréed strawberries
1   tablespoon honey
1   tablespoon lime juice

½   cup Pinot Gris
1   tablespoon unsalted Plugrá butter

COMBINE all ingredients except butter in a small saucepan and reduce by half. Finish by whisking in butter and reducing over medium-low heat until nappe.

# GREEN TEA ENCRUSTED AHI
## with Cucumber Salad and Lime Ginger Butter Sauce

This dish was created for the spring/summer 2006 menu. The idea behind it was to create a plate that was both light and clean on the palate while still being warm enough for a rainy NW spring. It is essential to this dish to use top grade (#1) tuna, as the cooking is minimal and the flavor of the fish itself is essential to the integrity of its flavor profile.

## Ingredients

24 ounces #1-grade ahi tuna loin, skin
   and bloodline removed
   salt to taste
   Green Tea Rub (recipe follows)
2 tablespoons pure olive oil

Cucumber Salad (recipe follows)
Lime Ginger Butter Sauce
daikon sprouts, pickled ginger, and
   sesame seeds for garnish

## Preparation

PREHEAT oven to 350 degrees. Cut tuna into 4 equal portions—block cuts if possible. Season fish on all sides with salt and roll in Green Tea Rub to coat.

HEAT oil in a medium sauté pan until almost smoking and sear tuna on all sides, 5 seconds per side. Remove from heat and set aside while you assemble the salad and make the sauce. When just about ready to serve, reheat the fish for 2 minutes in 350-degree oven, or to desired doneness.

TO SERVE, divide Cucumber Salad among 4 plates placing it at the 12 o'clock position on the plate. Slice each portion of tuna into 5 slices and fan out on plates in front of the salad. Drizzle with Lime Ginger Butter Sauce and garnish with daikon sprouts, pickled ginger, and sesame seeds.

*Serves 4*

*Wine Suggestion: 2005 Bunnell Family Cellars Gewürztraminer, Yakima Valley*

## For the Green Tea Rub

1 cup high quality loose-leaf green tea
¼ cup high quality loose-leaf citrus tea

1 tablespoon dried orange zest
1 tablespoon panko breadcrumbs

GRIND all ingredients in a coffee grinder or food processor until fine. Toss to evenly distribute ingredients.

## For the Cucumber Salad

- 2 English cucumbers, deseeded and diced
- ½ pint cherry tomatoes, halved
- ¼ cup daikon root, shredded
- 1 tablespoon sesame oil
- 1 tablespoon rice wine vinegar
- 1 tablespoon aji-mirin rice wine (a sweet cooking rice wine)

COMBINE all ingredients in a medium mixing bowl and toss to combine.

## For the Lime Ginger Butter Sauce

- 4 tablespoons key lime juice
- 4 tablespoons clover honey
- 12 slices pickled ginger
- 1 cup Pinot Gris
- 1 tablespoon unsalted Plugrá butter, or unsalted sweet butter

COMBINE all ingredients except the butter in a small saucepan over medium heat and reduce by half. Finish over low heat by whisking in butter and cooking until nappe.

# CORIANDER AND CITRUS CRUSTED ALASKAN HALIBUT
## with Herbed Risotto and White Peach Chardonnay Reduction

A guest favorite, this dish was a nightly special for most of the spring last year because of demand. So it only seemed logical to put it on the next menu, especially with the availability of halibut in the summer. It truly showcases one of the Northwest's greatest seafood treasures, and the white peach reduction just screams summer. I like to serve this dish with wilted Brussels sprout leaves, though any green vegetable will do.

## Ingredients

4 6-ounce portions fresh halibut filets
Coriander Citrus Rub (recipe follows)
salt and pepper to taste
2 tablespoons pure olive oil
Herb Risotto (recipe follows)

White Peach Chardonnay Reduction
(recipe follows)
green onion curls or flat leaf parsley,
for garnish

## Preparation

PREHEAT oven to 400 degrees. Coat presentation side of fish with Coriander Citrus Rub and season liberally with salt and pepper. Heat oil in a medium-sized sauté pan. Over high heat sear halibut, rubbed side down. Flip fish and transfer to oven for 5–7 minutes, depending on desired doneness.

TO SERVE, spoon Herb Risotto onto center of plate and top with fish and green vegetables. Spoon White Peach Chardonnay Reduction over the top of the fish and the plate. Garnish with green onion curls or flat leaf parsley.

*Serves 4*

*Wine Suggestion: 2004 Canoe Ridge Chardonnay, Columbia Valley*

## For the Coriander Citrus Rub

½ cup coriander seeds, lightly toasted
½ cup high quality loose-leaf chamomile
  tea

¼ cup orange zest
¼ cup lemon zest
¼ cup panko breadcrumbs

COMBINE all ingredients in food processor or coffee grinder and grind until fine, tossing to evenly distribute ingredients.

## For the White Peach Chardonnay Reduction

½ cup puréed white peaches
2 cups Chardonnay

1 tablespoon unsalted Plugrá butter, or unsalted sweet butter

COMBINE puréed peaches and wine in a small saucepan and reduce by half over medium-high heat. Finish over medium-low heat by whisking in butter and reducing to nappe.

## For the Herb Risotto

3 tablespoons unsalted Plugrá butter, or unsalted sweet butter
¼ cup sweet onion, diced
½ cup white wine
1 cup carnaroli rice
2½ cups chicken stock

1 pinch each fresh oregano, sage, rosemary, and chives
3 tablespoons Parmigiano Reggiano, shredded
salt and pepper to taste

IN A medium saucepan add 2 tablespoons of the butter and sweat onions over low heat, adding a pinch of salt and pepper to release some liquid. Deglaze with white wine and reduce by half. Add rice and stock and cook over medium-high heat, stirring constantly until almost all liquid is absorbed and rice has become tender. Add herbs and cheese, stirring to combine, and finish with remaining butter and salt and pepper to taste.

# APPLE PIE ALA MODE CHEESECAKE

This recipe was an idea that was conceived while I was in high school, though I could never get it quite right. The idea was to create a desert which was apple pie and ice cream together but easily presented, and in a unique manner. This past winter, our pastry chef Leia and I put our heads together and she managed to work out the kinks, adding a cobbler crust between the layers and breaking apple pie convention by cubing instead of slicing them. The cubing of the apples keeps them together better, so they don't slide when you cut into it, and the cobbler crust seals the layers and keeps them separate.

## Ingredients

| | |
|---|---|
| 1½ ounces cake flour | Apple Filling (recipe follows) |
| 4 ounces sugar | Pie Topping (recipe follows) |
| 4 ounces unsalted butter | Cheesecake Batter (recipe follows) |
| ½ tablespoon vanilla extract | caramel sauce |
| 2 eggs, whites and yolks separated | fresh apple slices for garnish |

## Preparation

PREHEAT oven to 350 degrees. Combine flour, sugar, butter, and vanilla in a large bowl and mix with hands until moist. Press into a greased 9-inch spring form pan. Brush egg whites over the top and perforate top with a fork. Bake in oven for 12–15 minutes and then cool in refrigerator until chilled, leaving spring-form pan in place. When chilled, press the Apple Filling into the chilled crust and place in refrigerator while making Pie Topping.

RAISE oven to 450 degrees. Place Pie Topping over chilled apple pie filling in the spring form pan and bake for 15–20 minutes, until golden brown and then cool.

LOWER oven temperature to 350 degrees. Pour Cheesecake Batter over cooled apple pie base in spring form pan. Bake for 1 hour in a water bath. Turn oven off and allow cake to rest for 1 hour with the oven door cracked. Cool cake overnight in the refrigerator. Remove the spring form pan the next day and cut with a hot knife. Serve with caramel sauce and garnish with fresh apple slices.

### Yield: 1cake

*Wine Suggestion: 2005 Silverlake late harvest Riesling, Columbia Valley*

## For the Apple Filling

| | |
|---|---|
| 2 large Fuji apples, ¼-inch dice | 2 tablespoons all-purpose flour |
| ¼ cup sugar | 1 teaspoon lemon juice |
| pinch salt | 2 tablespoons cinnamon |

COMBINE all ingredients in a bowl and mix to combine.

## For the Pie Topping

| | |
|---|---|
| 4 ounces pecans | pinch salt |
| 4 ounces oatmeal | 1 tablespoon cinnamon |
| 4 ounces granola | 2 egg whites |
| 8½ ounces cake flour | 6 ounces unsalted butter, cut in ¼-inch |
| 4 ounces sugar | cubes and chilled |
| 4 ounces packed brown sugar | |

BLEND pecans, oats, and granola in a food processor. Combine all ingredients except the butter and egg whites into mixer w/ paddle attachment and blend. Add cubed butter and mix for 1 minute on medium speed. Add egg whites one at a time on low speed. When mixture starts to crumble easily it is done.

## For the Cheesecake Batter

| | |
|---|---|
| 2 pounds cream cheese | 2 tablespoons flour |
| 1 pound sour cream | 1 vanilla bean, scraped and seeds |
| 8 ounces sugar | reserved |
| 3 eggs | pinch salt |

IN A mixer with paddle attachment, cream together the cream cheese and sour cream. Add sugar slowly and then add eggs, one at a time, allowing the mixture to come together. Add flour, vanilla bean seeds and salt, scraping the sides after each addition.

*By 1918, the railroad and the Sunset Highway brought tourists to Snoqualmie Falls. Some stayed at Snoqualmie Falls Lodge or stopped off to enjoy one of the lodge's famous breakfasts. Across the river from the lodge was the Puget Sound Power & Light Company's hydroelectric generating station, built in the 1890s. The electrical station is still there in the 1990s, but Salish Lodge now occupies the site of the old Snoqualmie Falls Lodge. Puget Power is now Puget Sound Energy. ca 1920*

# Salish Lodge

6501 Railroad Avenue SE
Snoqualmie, WA 98065
1-800-2-SALISH
425-888-2556
www.salishlodge.com

**Breakfast Monday – Friday**
7:00am – 11:00am
Saturday & Sunday 7:00am – 2:00pm
**Dinner Sunday, Tuesday – Thursday**
5:00pm – 9:00pm
Friday & Saturday 5:00pm – 10:00pm
**Reservations Highly Recommended**

# Salish Lodge

### Roy Breiman, Executive Chef
### Mark Kieras, Sommelier

A mere 30 miles east of Seattle, Salish Lodge & Spa is nestled in the foothills of the Cascade Mountains and perched near the world famous Snoqualmie Falls, which is considered by many to be a sacred place. Guests can still feel a chill as the sheer power of Mother Nature sends her emerald waters over the thundering falls only to disappear into mist hundreds of feet below. The first European settlers discovered the falls in 1851 and began running wagons from Seattle along logging roads to open up the natural wonder to the rest of society. The first lodge was built in 1916 as a food and rest stop to meet the needs of the influx of tourists. Walk into the present day Dining Room to view Salish's original fireplace and feast on the same traditional country breakfast that has been served for generations. In 1988, the building was completely remodeled and reopened as the Salish Lodge. In 1996, an award-winning spa was added to the premises, making Salish Lodge just as perfect for a one-day getaway as for a week vacation. Salish Lodge has three fabulous dining options: The Dining Room, The Attic Bistro, and The Kayak Café—all led by internationally-trained Executive Chef Roy Breiman. With his extensive experience working in top U.S. as well as Michelin-starred restaurants in Europe, Chef Roy has grown to appreciate the intricacies of carefully cultivated and lovingly raised foods.

Built around the original 1907 fireplace, The Dining Room serves Chef Roy's innovative cuisine, inspired by seasonal Northwest ingredients supplemented by the breathtaking views of the falls. Along with the inspired menu, you will find special menus featuring the cheeses of Herve Mons as well as a world chocolate menu. The Attic Bistro commands a bird's eye view of the falls and is a cozy place to unwind and experience more casual Salish-style dining. Featuring everything from steamed clams to steak tartar to the Attic's signature hot buttered rum it is sensationally indulgent. During summer, the outdoor bistro The Kayak Café, serves signature fare such as Seared Tuna Grilled Panini sandwiches, gourmet Salish Burgers and handcrafted Northwest brews.

The Dining Room at Salish Lodge has garnered many awards over the years, receiving the *Wine Spectator's Best of Award of Excellence* since 1988. It also received the 2006 *Award of Distinction* from *Wine Enthusiast* magazine. *Condé Nast Traveler* once again named the Salish Lodge to the *Gold List of World's Best* for 2007, one of only 168 resorts and hotels in the U.S. to receive this highly coveted award.

 Best of Award of Excellence

# BUTTERNUT SQUASH BISQUE
*with Maple Cinnamon Crème Fraîche, Toasted Almonds and Chervil*

## Ingredients

2 ounces butter

1 pound butternut squash, peeled and diced

6 ounces yellow onions, sliced

1 banana, sliced

1 Granny Smith apple, peeled, cored, and sliced

¼ cup brown sugar

4 cups chicken stock

1 Spice Sachet (recipe follows) salt to taste

6 ounces heavy cream

1 ounce almonds, sliced Cinnamon Crème Fraîche

4 sprigs chervil, for garnish

## Preparation

MELT butter in a medium-sized soup pot. Add butternut squash, onions, banana, and apple and cook over medium heat until all ingredients are well combined and turning translucent. Add brown sugar and cook until slightly browned and smelling of caramel. Add chicken stock, Spice Sachet, and season with salt. Reduce soup by half. Add heavy cream and reduce until soup has thickened. Remove sachet and blend until smooth. Keep warm until service. Preheat oven to 375 degrees. Place sliced almonds on a cookie sheet and toast in oven for approximately 8–10 minutes.

LADLE soup into warm soup bowls. Top soup with Cinnamon Crème Fraîche and toasted almonds and garnish with chervil sprigs.

*Serves 4*

## For the Spice Sachet

4 star anise

1 cinnamon stick

1 whole nutmeg, cracked

IN the center of a 12-inch by 12-inch piece of cheesecloth place the star anise, nutmeg, and cinnamon stick. Bring the corners together and wrap the top with butcher twine. Crack the spices with the back of the knife—this will release a more floral bouquet of spice for the soup.

## For the Cinnamon Crème Fraîche

2 ounces crème fraîche

¼ teaspoon ground cinnamon

½ ounce maple syrup

COMBINE the crème fraîche, ground cinnamon, and maple syrup into a mixing bowl. Mix until well incorporated and place in fridge for final presentation.

# Northwest Bouillabaisse

## Ingredients

| | |
|---|---|
| 1 liter (approx. 4 cups) Lobster Stock (recipe follows) | 8 scallops |
| 12 littleneck clams | 8 shrimp |
| 1 potato, diced and blanched | 4 ounces fresh wild salmon, cut in 1-inch pieces |
| ½ fennel bulb, sliced and blanched | 8 ounces white fish (halibut or Alaskan black cod), cut in 1-inch pieces |
| ½ green zucchini, sliced | Potato-Saffron Rouille (recipe follows) |
| ½ yellow zucchini, sliced | parsley or chervil, for garnish (optional) |
| 12 pearl onions, peeled and blanched | croutons (optional) |
| 6 garlic cloves, chopped | |
| 1 teaspoon thyme, chopped | |
| 1 bay leaf | |

## Preparation

IN A medium pot, large enough to hold all ingredients easily, heat to boil the Lobster Stock. Add littleneck clams and cook for 2 minutes. Combine diced potato, fennel, zucchini, pearl onions, garlic, thyme, and bay leaf and add to pot. Under a slow boil continue to cook an additional 2 minutes. Add scallops, shrimp, salmon, and white fish. Lower heat to simmer and cook until fish is lightly poached.

TO SERVE, place bouillabaisse ingredients into large serving bowls adding enough broth to each, as appropriate. Add several teaspoons of Potato-Saffron Rouille. Garnish with parsley, chervil, and croutons as desired and serve immediately.

*Serves 4*

*Wine Suggestion: For fun, try a French Bandol or a Côtes du Rhone. A sassy Zinfandel with heavy earth tones and a scent of wild herbs would also work well.*

## For the Lobster Stock

| | |
|---|---|
| 4 pounds lobster bodies | 1 bunch fresh thyme |
| 2 ounces olive oil | 1 whole garlic, cut with skin on |
| 1 carrot, chopped | 2 bay leaves |
| 1 onion, chopped | 1 cup white wine |
| 2 fresh tomatoes | 3 cups chicken stock |
| 1 celery stalk, chopped | salt & pepper |

PREHEAT oven to 450 degrees. Coat lobster bodies with olive oil, place in a roasting pan and cook in preheated oven until well browned and smelling of roast shellfish. Remove from oven and add carrot, onion, tomatoes, celery, thyme, garlic, and bay leaves to pan and cook an additional 10 minutes. Remove pan from oven and transfer ingredients to a large saucepot.

Add white wine, and reduce by 75%. Add chicken stock and reduce by 50%. Pass broth through a strainer and vigorously press shells to extract the maximum amount of flavor from the lobster. Discard solids.

## For Potato-Saffron Rouille

| | |
|---|---|
| 1  potato, cooked, and puréed | 1  small pinch of saffron |
| 3  tomatoes, peeled, seeded, and chopped | 1  cup olive oil |
| 6  garlic cloves, chopped | salt & pepper to taste |
| 1  shallot, chopped | |

PLACE potato purée, tomatoes, garlic, shallot, and saffron into a stainless steel mixing bowl, mix thoroughly. Slowly combine olive oil while whisking. Season with salt and pepper and hold for service.

# LAYERS OF FRESH AND SMOKED SALMON
### with Toasted Brioche and Caviar Butter

## Ingredients

6  1-ounce circles Toasted Brioche
   (recipe follows)
12  ounces smoked salmon, thinly sliced
12  ounces fresh salmon, thinly sliced

½  pound Caviar Butter (recipe follows)
6  cherry tomatoes, sliced in half
6  parsley sprigs, for garnish

## Preparation

PREHEAT oven to 475 degrees. In the center of a large 12-inch ovenproof serving plate, place the circles of Toasted Brioche.  On top of each brioche arrange a 2-ounce ruffled layer of smoked salmon. On top of smoked salmon, arrange a 2-ounce ruffled layer of fresh salmon. Place in oven until fresh salmon turns a light shade of pink. Remove from oven and spoon 2 tablespoons Caviar Butter on top of each. Garnish with tomatoes and parsley and serve immediately.

### Serves 6

*Wine Suggestion: A big and buttery Chardonnay with a slight tinge of oak and nice accents of stone fruit.*

## For Caviar Butter

¾  pound whole butter
1  ounce black caviar (American
   sturgeon, osetra)

1  ounce salmon caviar

PLACE whole butter in saucepan over medium heat and slowly bring to a boil. Skim butterfat off top until contents have been clarified. Place clarified butter in separate container, letting it cool to room temperature. Add caviar to butter. Set aside for final presentation.

## For Toasted Brioche

brioche bread
2  tablespoons clarified butter

salt to taste

CUT 6 circles from the brioche, each 3 inches in diameter. In a sauté pan, heat clarified butter over medium heat. Lightly cook brioche circles on both sides until golden brown. Season with salt. Remove, pat dry, and set aside for final presentation.

# SKAGIT VALLEY DUCK BREAST
## *with Wild Mushrooms and Cabernet Fig Sauce*

## Ingredients

5 tablespoons butter, divided
⅓ cup shallots, finely chopped
1 pound wild mushrooms (such as portobello, chanterelle, oyster, and stemmed shiitake), thinly sliced
1 teaspoon fresh ginger, finely chopped
¼ cup chicken stock
3 tablespoons fresh chives, chopped

16 Black Mission figs (fresh or dried)
¼ cup honey
2 boneless duck breasts, with skin (all natural)
salt & pepper to taste
1 tablespoon olive oil
Cabernet Fig Sauce (recipe follows)
fresh chives for garnish (optional)

## Preparation

MELT 4 tablespoons of the butter in heavy large skillet over medium-high heat. Add shallots and sauté until translucent, about 4 minutes. Add mushrooms and ginger; sauté until mushrooms are tender, about 4 minutes. Add chicken stock and simmer until most of liquid is evaporated, about 4 minutes. Stir in chopped chives. Keep warm.

PREHEAT oven to 450 degrees. Place figs in small glass baking dish and drizzle honey over figs. Bake in oven until figs are tender and honey is slightly caramelized, about 12 minutes.

MEANWHILE, sprinkle duck breasts with salt and pepper. Melt remaining 1 tablespoon of butter with olive oil in another heavy large skillet over medium heat. Add duck breasts, skin side down, and cook 5 minutes. Turn duck breasts over and continue cooking to desired doneness, about 3 minutes for medium-rare.

TO SERVE, spoon mushrooms into center of each plate, dividing equally. Slice duck breasts and arrange atop mushrooms. Reheat Cabernet Fig Sauce—if made a day in advance—and spoon over duck. Place 4 caramelized figs on each plate. Garnish with chives, if desired.

### *Serves 4*

*Wine Suggestion: A 100% Cabernet would be fabulous, or a Merlot, or a nice Bourdeaux-style wine with hints of cinnamon and wild berries.*

## For the Cabernet Fig Sauce

14 Black Mission figs (fresh or dried)
2 cups Cabernet wine

2 cups chicken stock
2 cinnamon sticks

CUT figs in half lengthwise. Combine cut figs, wine, chicken stock, and cinnamon sticks in medium saucepan. Simmer over medium-high heat until thickened to sauce consistency, stirring occasionally, about 30 minutes. Strain sauce, pressing on solids to release juices. Discard solids. This sauce can be prepared 1 day ahead, if covered and chilled.

# Warm Chocolate Tart with Vanilla Ice Cream

## Ingredients

1 cup heavy cream
8 ounces bittersweet chocolate (72% cocoa content), chopped in pieces

4 Tart Shells (recipe follows)
4 scoops of vanilla ice cream
4 sprigs fresh mint, for garnish

## Preparation

HEAT cream to a slow boil using a double boiler. Whisk in chocolate until it has melted and is well combined. Remove from stove and let cool for 5 minutes.

ADD chocolate mixture to the previously made Tart Shells and let rest at room temperature an additional hour, to let the chocolate cool and set.

WHEN ready to serve, arrange on a serving plate and garnish with ice cream and mint and serve immediately.

*Serves 4*

## For the Tart Shells

5 ounces sugar
1 pound flour

11 ounces butter, softened
1 egg

SIFT together the sugar and flour and make a well on a clean surface. Place the butter and egg in the center of the well. Slowly combine the flour from the perimeter into the butter and egg mixture. Once all the flour has been incorporated, work the dough manually until smooth in texture. Wrap in plastic wrap and let rest in refrigerator for 1 hour.

PREHEAT oven to 325 degrees. Remove dough from fridge and place on a clean surface that's been lightly floured. Using a rolling pin, roll out dough to ⅛-inch thickness. Cut circles and place in a buttered ring. Bake dough rings in 325-degree oven until slightly brown, approximately 10 minutes. Remove and let rest.

# Inna's Cuisine

26 N. Wenatchee Avenue
Wenatchee, WA 98801
509-888-4662
www.innascuisine.com

Open Monday – Saturday
11:00am – 9:00pm

# Inna's Cuisine

### *Inna Kazulina, Chef/Owner*

The story of Inna's Cuisine is a heart-warming narrative of hard work, unique ability, and the drive to achieve the American dream. The result shows in the lovely European restaurant in the heart of downtown Wenatchee. A Ukrainian native, Inna Kazulina immigrated to America with her husband, Sergiy Kazulin, in 1998. They did not come as refugees, but because Sergiy had won a visa through a lottery that allows people to move to the United States, receive a green card, and apply for U.S. citizenship. They came to this country with educations, careers, and a business plan. Inna graduated from International Cooking School in 1983, and graduated from Kharkiv University of Ukraine in 1990. She worked for the Black Sea Company on passenger cruise ships and has a total of over twenty years experience in the culinary arts.

Owning her own restaurant was a long-held dream for Inna. Shortly after moving to America, Inna and Sergiy purchased the Coffee Depot, a 300-square foot business at 7 N. Wenatchee Avenue. Along with the regular muffins, rolls, and sandwiches found in most coffee shops, Inna served pirogues and borscht to her customers. The business was so successful that the couple had to look for larger quarters to execute the next step in their business plan—a full scale European restaurant. The perfect opportunity presented itself just a few steps down the street. Sergiy and Inna purchased the 104-year-old Brissette building in 2005. A large mural portraying a small French town that had been painted by local artist, Harrell Shrammer, decorated one of the walls of the new restaurant space. The mural was kept as part of the décor, which also features a romantic mezzanine for just a couple of tables and a third floor loft area from which you can look down upon the entire restaurant. The charming and elegant atmosphere of the restaurant is enhanced with crisp ivory linen tablecloths and burgundy napkins, along with sparkling wine glasses.

Chef Inna's cooking, however, is the heart of the restaurant, with meals influenced by Greek, Italian, Russian, and Ukrainian cuisine. Many of Inna's customers have European roots, and remember the food that their grandmothers and mothers made for them, bringing back memories of home. Others who have traveled in Europe are delighted to find some of the culinary delicacies they enjoyed in their travels. Along with the wonderful ethnic cuisine, Inna offers a wide variety of wines and beers. The wine list features many Washington wineries, as well as wines from France, Italy, Ukraine, Georgia, Moldavia, and Germany. The beers include many American favorites, along with six different varieties of Baltika, the largest and most popular of the Russian beers.

# STUFFED MUSHROOMS

## Ingredients

| | |
|---|---|
| 12 medium-size white mushrooms | ½ pound bacon, diced |
| 1 medium yellow onion, diced | 2 celery stalks, sliced thinly |
| olive oil | 1 pound Gorgonzola cheese |

## Preparation

PREHEAT oven to 425 degrees. Remove stems of mushrooms and put mushroom caps upside down on a baking sheet.

SAUTÉ onion with olive oil until gold. Add bacon and cook until crisp, about 5 minutes. Add celery and cook 2 more minutes. Remove from heat and let cool. Stuff the mushroom caps with this mixture and cover stuffed mushrooms with cheese. Bake in 425-degree oven for 8–10 minutes, until cheese has melted and mushrooms are tender.

*Serves 4*

*Wine Suggestion: Merlot Saint Laurent*

# Katherine' Linguine

## Ingredients

1 pound dry linguine
12 ounces mushrooms, sliced
24 prawns (16/20 size), peeled
4 tablespoons garlic, chopped
1 teaspoon garlic salt
½ cup olive oil

5 ounces white wine
1 ounce lemon juice
1 quart heavy whipping cream (30%)
½ cup Parmesan cheese, shredded
1 tablespoon fresh parsley, chopped

## Preparation

BRING a large pot of water to boil and cook pasta until it is al dente. In a large pan, cook mushrooms, prawns, garlic, and garlic salt for 5 minutes. Add white wine and lemon juice and cook another minute. Add heavy cream and Parmesan cheese and cook for 2 minutes. Add linguine and parsley and cook 5 minutes, stirring all the time. Serve immediately.

*Serves 4*

*Wine Suggestion: Very good with Riesling or Pinot Gris Chateau Faire Le Pont*

# Arrabiata Salmon with Inna's Special Sauce

## Ingredients

4　7-ounce portions wild Alaskan king
　salmon
　Arrabiata Mix (recipe follows)

　spring lettuce mix
　Inna's Special Sauce (recipe follows)

## Preparation

PREHEAT oven to 425 degrees. Season each portion of salmon with Arrabiata Mix and place on a baking sheet. Bake in oven for 5 minutes, or an internal temperature of 145 degrees is achieved.

SERVE salmon over spring lettuce mix and top with Inna's Special Sauce. This is lovely served with mashed potatoes and a medley of sautéed vegetables.

*Serves 4*

*Wine Suggestion: Very good with Provence or Confluence Chateau Fair Le Pont*

## For the Arrabiata Mix

3　cups brown sugar
¼　cup dry basil
½　cup cayenne pepper

¼　cup ground black pepper
1　cup paprika

MIX all ingredients together to combine.

## For Inna's Special Sauce

1　cup mayonnaise
1　cup sour cream
1　red bell pepper, finely chopped

6–8　fresh basil leaves, slice
½　teaspoon salt
2　tablespoons lemon juice

MIX all ingredients together and hold for service.

# Golubtzi (Cabbage Rolls) in Tomato Sauce

## Ingredients

16  cabbage leaves, still attached to
    cabbage head
2  cups yellow onion, finely chopped
2  cups carrots, finely shredded
1  pound ground beef
2  tablespoons parsley

1  tablespoon dill
1  teaspoon Mrs. Dash® seasoning
1  teaspoon salt
    Tomato Sauce (recipe follows)
    sour cream

## Preparation

BRING a large pot of water to a boil and put cabbage in to boil for 5 minutes. Separate leaves from head when they start to soften. Take from water and cool. Cut off hard stem to release individual leaves.

PREHEAT oven to 375 degrees. Sauté onions in olive oil for 7 minutes, then add carrots and cook for 3 more minutes. In a bowl, mix the ground beef, parsley, dill, Mrs. Dash®, and salt with the sautéed onions and carrots. Stuff cabbage leaves with the mix and roll them up. Place leaves seam side down in a baking pan. Cover cabbage rolls with Tomato Sauce and bake in oven for 1 hour, 25 minutes.

SERVE with sour cream.

### Serves 15

*Wine Suggestion: Very good with Merlot, Saint Lauren or Georgian wine, Khvanchra.*

# Cake "Napoleon"

## Ingredients

11 ounces softened butter
11 ounces sour cream
½ teaspoon salt
2 tablespoons sugar

15 tablespoons flour
2 eggs, beaten
"Napoleon" Cream Filling (recipe follows)

## Preparation

COMBINE butter, sour cream, salt, sugar, flour, and eggs to make dough. Divide dough into 12 pieces and shape into balls. Let dough rest in refrigerator for 1 hour.

PREHEAT oven to 400 degrees. Roll out each piece of dough to a very thin sheet. It can be either round or square shaped. Trim off any extra so that all 12 sheets are exactly the same size. Combine the trimmings into 1 or 2 sheets and roll out to same thinness. These are to be crushed and used for top of cake, so they do not have to be the same size as the 12 sheets.

BAKE all sheets in 400-degree oven for 1–2 minutes, or until gold in color. Cool baked sheets.

WHEN sheets have cooled, place 1 sheet on a serving tray. Using a spoon, spread some of the "Napoleon" Cream Filling on top of the sheet. Place second layer on top of the cream and spread more cream on top of this layer. Repeat process until all 12 layers are assembled, with cream on the top layer. Crush the extra 2 sheets and use them to decorate the top of the cake. Allow cake to sit at room temperature for 4–6 hours, and then keep in refrigerator.

*Serves 16*

## For the "Napoleon" Cream Filling

5 egg yolks
2 cups sugar
1 teaspoon vanilla extract

6 tablespoons flour
4 cups 2% milk

MIX egg yolks with sugar and vanilla until creamy. Add flour and mix again. Very slowly, add 1 cup of the milk and mix well. Mixture should be consistent. Place remaining 3 cups of milk in a pot on heat and bring to a boil. Add mixture and stir constantly until it comes back to a boil. Remove from heat and cool.

*Yakima County is still a center for the tree fruit industry. Irrigation efforts started in the 1870s, and by 1907, area orchards were producing apples, cherries, pears, peaches, plums, prunes, and apricots. About two million young fruit trees were planted in 1906 and early 1907 alone. ca 1911*

# Capers

## Fine Dining

127 East Johnson Avenue
Chelan, WA 98816
509-682-1611
www.capersfinedining.com

Dinner Wednesday through
Monday from 6:00pm

# Capers Fine Dining

### Hendrika Isensee, Chef/Owner

The beautiful Lake Chelan area of Washington offers so much to tourists and residents alike. The name Chelan comes from the Native American word for deep water, and rightly so. Lake Chelan is one of the deepest lakes in North America. Its cool, clear waters are a boon to those who love water sports and fishing; not to mention just the enjoyment of relaxing by the shore and gazing at the emerald waters and pine-covered mountains.

The inviting little town of Chelan at the southern tip of Lake Chelan provides a perfect base for those who come to enjoy the lake as well as to tour the growing number of wineries that have been established in the area. After an active day, both visitors and locals who enjoy the relaxing experience of fine dining have a special treat in store at Capers.

The tan nondescript building with the dark green trim on East Johnson Avenue belies the classical surroundings and comfortable atmosphere that you will find on the inside. Hendrika Isensee has created a charming restaurant with a European ambience that has been called, "Chelan's most elegant restaurant." Upholstered armchairs, crisp linen, and fresh flowers add to the special feeling of the restaurant.

A native of Holland, Hendrika immigrated to British Columbia, where she honed her culinary skills in the catering industry for about 25 years. After purchasing a ranch in the Chelan area, she saw a need for a fine dining restaurant. Starting Capers a little over five years ago, her primary goal was to please her customers. She and her headwaiter, Colby, bend over backward to accommodate special requests. Hendrika says that she has gone so far as to receive a customer's "catch of the day" to prepare special dishes—grouse, steelhead, truffles, etc. Although the menu is changed twice a year, it is not unusual for her to create special dishes for longtime patrons.

Capers menu usually sports the classic European fare such as Chateaubriand and Duck 'a L'Orange, but it also offers unusual dishes. Such delectable items as rabbit simmered in Cabernet Sauvignon, Dungeness crab cakes served with a maple chipotle aioli, and seared venison loin deglazed with Port and topped with morel and chanterelle mushrooms often appear on the menu.

Chef Hendrika especially enjoys creating dishes for the Winemakers Dinners that she occasionally hosts. With twelve wineries in the area, she tries to feature the local wines. The wine list features 120 items, more than half of which are from the Northwest.

# CAPERS SIGNATURE POPPY SEED SALAD

## Ingredients

2 heads of butter lettuce
1 avocado, sliced
1 cup canned Mandarin orange sections
¼ red onion, very thinly sliced

½ cup toasted almonds
1 cup Poppy Seed Dressing (recipe below)

## Preparation

WASH and pat dry the butter lettuce leaves and arrange on plates. Arrange avocado slices and onion slices on top and drizzle with Poppy Seed Dressing. Top with orange segments and sprinkle with almonds.

*Serves 4*

## For the Poppy Seed Dressing

1 large egg
½ cup champagne vinegar
½ cup red wine vinegar
½ cup red wine
2 shallots, chopped fine

½ cup sugar
2 teaspoons salt
1 teaspoon Dijon mustard
1¾ cups canola oil
¼ cup poppy seeds

PUT all ingredients in blender except poppy seeds and canola oil. Blend well and then add canola oil in small stream to emulsify the mixture. Stir in poppy seeds.

# TOMATO BASIL SOUP

Not an ordinary tomato basil soup, due to some "secret" ingredients that I am happy to reveal.

## Ingredients

1   large can of pear tomato sauce
1   cup of roasted garlic, roughly chopped
1   cup Parmesan cheese, grated
1   cup Cabernet Sauvignon
2   cups fresh basil, julienned
2   teaspoons Maggi® (Swiss seasoning available in larger grocery outlets)

4   teaspoons ketjap manis (Oriental sweet soy sauce)
6   teaspoons brown sugar
2   cups chicken stock
4   cups heavy cream

## Preparation

STIR all ingredients together and refrigerate overnight to allow all flavors to absorb into the sauce. Reheat gently over low heat, stirring frequently.

*Serves 12*

# GRUYERE STUFFED CHICKEN IN PHYLLO

An elegant way to treat a simple chicken breast. Fresh basil and slices of sun-dried tomatoes give added flavor while the phyllo makes for a great presentation. Drizzle with Red Bell Pepper Aioli.

## Ingredients

- 1  breast chicken, skinless and boneless
- 3  sheets phyllo pastry
- 2  large fresh basil leaves
- 2  slices sun-dried tomatoes in olive oil
- 1  1½-ounce slice of Gruyere cheese
   (Asiago can be substituted)

clarified butter to sauté chicken
melted putter for phyllo
salt& pepper to taste
Red Bell Pepper Aioli (recipe follows)

## Preparation

PREHEAT oven to 350 degrees. Cut a slice in the thick part of the chicken breast—sufficiently large to allow the cheese, basil, and tomato to be inserted. Salt and pepper the breast and sauté it in clarified butter until almost completely done (until juices run clear or cheese starts to run). Tent and set aside. At this point chicken can be stored cold until ready for use.

BUTTER each phyllo sheet with melted butter and place on top of each other. Place chicken in the middle of one side of the phyllo sheets and roll the phyllo around the chicken. Place the wrap in a cake pan so that the ends of the phyllo rest on the sides and point up.

BAKE in 350-degree oven until phyllo is light brown. Slice the phyllo package at an angle and rest one piece upon the other. Drizzle with Red Pepper Aioli and serve.

*Serves 1*

## For the Red Bell Pepper Aioli

- ½  roasted red bell pepper, seeded
- 1  teaspoon canned chipotle pepper

1  teaspoon mayonnaise
1  teaspoon maple syrup

PLACE all ingredients in blender and blend until smooth. Hold for service.

# LOIN OF VENISON
*with Morel and Button Mushrooms*

Rated by our customers as "the best venison dish ever," It is extremely simple and fast to prepare. We recommend serving the venison quite rare.

## Ingredients

1  4-oounce short loin of Cervena (New
   Zealand venison)
   salt & pepper to taste
4  morel mushrooms
4  button mushrooms
4  cloves roasted garlic, diced

1  ounce ruby Port
1  ounce demi-glace (can substitute beef
   broth or stock)
   clarified butted to sauté
1  cup long grain and wild rice, cooked

## Preparation

SAUTÉ salted and peppered venison in hot clarified butter, until outside is brown. Immediately add mushrooms and sauté briefly, then add garlic. Deglaze with port, add demi-glace, and lower heat. Cook a few minutes longer to the desired doneness. Venison should not be overcooked.

AFTER "resting" the venison, slice into ¼-inch slices and fan over wild and long grain rice.

TOP with mushrooms and sauce.

*Serves 1*

# Meringue Supreme

This desert is my personal favorite.

## Ingredients

- 4  egg whites at room temperature
- 1  teaspoon vanilla extract
- 1  cup finely sifted sugar
   parchment paper

- good quality ice cream
- whipped cream
- Chocolate Topping  (recipe follows)

## Preparation

PREHEAT oven to 250 degrees. In a non-reactive bowl, beat egg whites until foamy. Add vanilla. Now add sugar in small quantities—¼ cup at a time—until mixture forms stiff peaks. Place mixture in a piping bag and pipe onto parchment-covered baking sheet to form a base. With a tablespoon, press a hollow into the center. Bake in 250-degree oven until set and completely dry, but do not allow meringue to brown. (Meringues can be stored almost indefinitely in an airtight container.)

WHEN meringue has cooled, place ice cream on meringue base and top with whipped cream. Drizzle with Chocolate Topping.

*Serves 8*

## For the Chocolate Topping

- 4  ounces high quality baking chocolate (60 % plus cocoa)
- ½  cup heavy cream

CHOP chocolate and place in the top of a double boiler over boiling water. When melted, add the cream until incorporated. Keep warm for service.

*Interior of a Northern Pacific Railway dining car.  Febuary 10, 1923*

# Tendrils
## at Sagecliffe

**TENDRILS**
AT SAGECLIFFE

Cave B Inn
344 Silica Road NW
Quincy, WA 98950
509-785-2283
www.cavebinn.com

Open seven days a week for
Breakfast, Lunch, and Dinner
Reservations Required for
Dinner on Weekends

# Tendrils at SageCliffe

### *Fernando Divina, Executive Chef*
### *Shauna Scriver, Chef de Cuisine*
### *Dane Rice, Sous Chef*

The SageCliffe complex on a remote cliff overlooking the mighty Columbia River has become a destination in itself. Dr. Vince Bryan and his wife, Carol, created a unique retreat that is the Pacific Northwest's first luxury wine resort. The complex consists of the Cave B Estate Winery, Cave B Inn, and The Spa at Sage-Cliffe, and is located just north of Interstate 90 on the eastern cliffs of the Columbia River.

The winery released its first wines in 2000. Guests and visitors can enjoy a taste of the Cave B Estate wines in an intimate tasting room featuring a 17-foot tasting bar, handcrafted by local artisans from aged French oak wine barrel staves.

The Cave B Inn features fifteen private "Cliffhouses" and twelve "Cavern Lofts" as well as guest suites in the main lodge. All are architecturally designed to blend in with the natural environment of the sage-covered cliffs and most offer sweeping views of the sky, water, and canyon. The main lodge features soaring ceilings and locally crafted iron-turned chandeliers along with Tendrils, a warm and inviting restaurant. As Director for the Center for American Food and Wine at SageCliffe and as Executive Chef and Manager of Tendrils, Fernando Divina offers foods that are local, natural, organic, humanely raised, or are from ecologically sound farms and ranches within the region. He views the cuisine that he and his team have created as a "work in progress balancing the virtues of local food stuffs with nature's habit of delivering variable results." The Chef's on-site organic test orchards, culinary gardens, and herb gardens contribute to the enjoyment of many gastronomic creations that are artfully paired with Cave B Estate wines. The restaurant also has a wine tasting bar, a culinary demonstration kitchen, and a beautiful fireside lounge.

Chef Divina and has staff are inspired by the ancient origins of food, but strive for a contemporary presentation, always looking to local ingredients for inspiration. He published his own cookbook, *Food of the Americas: Native Recipes and Traditions*, which he co-authored with his wife, Marlene. He received the award for best book in the category of "Food of the Americas" from the esteemed *James Beard Foundation*. Chef Divina's long-standing commitment to the use of regional produce and purveyors has dovetailed with the Slow Food Movement. In 2000, he was nominated by international jurors for the prestigious Slow Food Award.

# CHERRY VINAIGRETTE

This is a terrific way to utilize less than perfect cherries. Combine fresh aggressive greens like dandelion, lambs quarter, or watercress with sweet lettuces like butter and Bibb varieties to balance the salad. The addition of sun-dried cherries or other dried fruits and toasted hazelnuts adds texture and an opportunity to improvise. Try substituting plums, peaches, or even berries for the cherries as variations.

## Ingredients

½ cup cherries, seeds removed
  juice of ¼ lemon
2 tablespoons sherry or champagne
  vinegar

½ cup hazelnut or walnut oil
pinch sea or course salt
  freshly ground black pepper

## Preparation

PLACE cherries in a food processor or blender. Pulse the cherries, adding a little oil at a time, until the cherries are liquefied. Add the lemon juice and vinegar to the processor and pulse 2–3 times. Add salt and pepper and toss with greens or serve on the side. This vinaigrette is best when served immediately and at room temperature.

*Yield: about ⅔ cup, enough for about 4–6 salads*

*Wine Suggestion: Serve this salad with chilled Cave B Estate Blanc de Blanc or Gewürztraminer.*

# CHILLED MELON SOUP
## *with Sparkling Wine and Mint Ice*

With the reintroduction of vibrantly colored and tasty heirloom melons, many gardens in temperate zones that allow for proper ripening now yield luscious varieties. Paired with two of Eastern Washington's premier ingredients—mint and sparkling wine—your surplus melons are transformed into this simple and elegant soup. Prepare the ice up to a few days ahead of time for convenience. Try serving the soup in chilled melon halves with the shaved ice and mint sprays accompanied by crunchy crackers, sliced cured meat, and dessert for a light luncheon.

## Ingredients

- 1  ripe melon, Cantaloupe, Crenshaw, Sheryln, or your favorite melon
- 1  cup water, more or less, depending on desired consistency
- 1  teaspoon coarse salt
- 2  dashes hot pepper sauce

- 1  teaspoon dry mustard
- 1–2  tablespoons honey (optional)
   Sparkling Wine and Mint Ice (recipe follows)
- 4  mint sprays, for garnish

## Preparation

WASH the melon and pat dry with a towel. Peel, seed, and coarsely chop the melon. Place the chopped melon in a food processor, blender, or food mill. Liquefy the melon in batches if necessary, transferring the processed purée to a bowl. With a whisk, stir in up to 1 cup of the water, adjusting the thickness of the purée as you desire. Stir the salt, hot pepper sauce, and mustard into the purée.

TASTE and add some or all of the optional honey, if desired. Feel free to add more of the other ingredients to suit your taste as well. Cover the soup and refrigerate until you are ready to serve, up to 2–3 hours prior to service. While this soup benefits from allowing some time for the flavors to "ripen", like most fruit-based dishes, this soup is best served within hours of preparation and only slightly chilled.

TO SERVE, ladle the soup into decorative frozen cups or hollowed melon. Remove the Sparkling Wine and Mint Ice from freezer and place in soup. If frozen in ice cubes, place several in each serving or, if frozen in a sheet, break pieces of the sheet up and place in each serving. Garnish with a spray of fresh mint.

*Yield: about 1 quart*

## For the Sparkling Wine and Mint Ice

- 1  tablespoon shallot, minced
- ¼  cup mint leaves, loosely packed, chiffonade

- 6  ounces sparkling wine
- 1  pinch black pepper, freshly ground

PLACE all ingredients in a bowl and stir with a fork to combine. You can freeze in ice cube trays or a shallow plastic tray, shaped to your preference.

# SageCliffe Gourmet
# Apple Sauce and Hazelnut Muffins

The SageCliffe Gourmet Apple Sauce rings true to its flavors and to the folks at SageCliffe. Our joy of place rings through with the deep, resonant apple flavors with a touch of apple blossom and sage honey taken from the bees that serve to pollinate our crops. Then to balance, the sauce was lightly acidulated and appended with a layer of chardonnay grape juice pressed by our winemaker and finally, with simple alchemy in the kitchen at the hearth of Team Tendrils.

These muffins can also be made into tiny muffins and served as one of an assortment in a basket of warm quick breads. Just omit the topping.

## Ingredients

- 1½ cups all-purpose flour
- 1½ teaspoons baking powder
- ½ teaspoon baking soda
- ½ teaspoon ground cinnamon or canela
- ¼ teaspoon ground allspice
- ¼ teaspoon grated mace
- ¼ teaspoon salt
- 2 large eggs

- 1 cup loosely packed light brown sugar
- 1 stick (½ cup) plus 3 tablespoons unsalted butter, melted
- 1 cup SageCliffe Gourmet Apple Sauce ™
- ¾ cup hazelnuts (2¾ oz), toasted, peeled and coarsely chopped
- Muffin Topping (recipe follows)

## Preparation

ADJUST oven rack to middle position and preheat oven to 375°F. Grease a 12-muffin pan. Stir together flour, baking powder, baking soda, spices, and salt in a bowl. Whisk together eggs and brown sugar in a bowl until well combined, then add butter in small pieces whisking between each addition until the mixture is creamy. Stir in applesauce, then fold in flour mixture with a rubber spatula until flour is just moistened, do not over mix. Fold in the nuts and distribute the batter into the prepared muffin pan.

SPRINKLE Muffin Topping on top of muffins and bake until muffins are golden, about 20 minutes. Cool in pan on a rack 5–7 minutes, then remove muffins from pan and serve.

### Yield: 12 muffins

*Wine Suggestion: Serve these muffins for Sunday breakfast with Cave B Blanc de Blanc or Cave B Sémillon Ice Wine and some ruffled ham.*

## For the Muffin Topping

- 1¾ tablespoons turbinado or white sugar
- ¼ teaspoon ground cinnamon or canela

- ⅛ teaspoon ground allspice
- ⅛ teaspoon mace

STIR together all topping ingredients in a bowl until well combined.

# STRAIT OF SAN JUAN BRODETTO

This brightly flavored dish takes its queue from the Iberian Peninsula, Spain and her cooks where the Pacific Northwest shoreline was among the touchstones of "first contact" that forever after influenced the cookery of the region. Add your local fish and shellfish and use a dry wine of your region to personalize this splendid dish.

## Ingredients

- 1 tablespoon olive oil
- 1 tablespoon shallot, minced
- 1 pinch saffron threads
- 1 pinch crumbled, dry chiles
- 4 2-ounce pieces of shellfish sausage, or substitute your favorite sausage
- 1 dozen clams (about 12–16 ounces total)
- 1 dozen small mussels (about 8 ounces total)
- ¼ cup dry white wine, such as 2004 Cave B Semillon

- ½ cup clam juice
- ½ cup water
- 1 cup chicken broth
- 1 tablespoon sweet pepper, ¼-inch dice
- 1 tablespoon fennel, ¼-inch dice
- 1 tablespoon roasted, peeled, and seeded tomato, ¼-inch dice
- sea salt, or substitute a salt that best suits your taste
- freshly ground black pepper
- fennel tops, for garnish

## Preparation

PREHEAT a cataplana (a pan of Portuguese origin used throughout the Mediterranean to steam fish and shellfish) or heavy pot with its tight fitting lid over medium high heat. Remove the lid then add the oil. Cook the shallot, stirring and without browning, for 1 minute. Add the saffron, chilies, and sausage. Brown the sausages without cooking too long, as you will finish cooking them with the shellfish a bit later in the cooking process. Remove the browned sausages with a spoon to a warm spot. Reserve the undercooked sausages while completing the brodetto.

ADD the clams, mussels, wine, clam juice, water, and chicken broth to the pan. Cover the pot tightly and steam for about 4–7 minutes or until the clams and mussels open. Add the reserved sausage, the sweet pepper, fennel, and tomato. Cover the pot tightly for 2–3 minutes or until the sausage is cooked through and the vegetables are heated but not soft. Taste the broth and add a pinch of sea salt and pepper if needed. Garnish sparingly with a few fennel tops and serve immediately with slices of crusty bread.

### Serves 4 as a small course

*Wine Suggestion: Cave B Estate Semillon*

# Greystone

## Greystone

5 N. Front Street    Lunch
Yakima, WA 98901    Monday – Friday from 11:30am
509-248-9801    Dinner
www.greystonedining.com    Monday – Saturday from 5:00pm

# Greystone Restaurant

## Mark and Lori Strosahl, Proprietors

Situated in the heart of Yakima's newly renovated Historic Front Street District, Greystone Restaurant occupies the ground floor of the Lund Building, which is on the National Register of Historic Places. Erected in 1899, the building faces the Union Pacific railroad terminal. Pictures of the area show the Lund Building circa 1907, when a trolley system was built using the railroad terminal as its starting point and extending out into the West Valley and Wiley City areas. The trolley was built to help transport workers—some living in the apartments in the Lund Building—to the apple orchards. On its return, the trolley and rail system transported apples back to the warehouses located along the Union Pacific siding in downtown Yakima. This area was referred to as Fruit Row.

There has been a restaurant or saloon located in the Lund Building as far back as can be verified. The first know name of a saloon in the building was the Alfalfa Saloon, which had been in existence for some time in 1933. After various saloons and restaurants occupied the building, proprietors Nancy Beveridge and Gayla Games opened the Greystone Restaurant in 1983, and operated the venture until Greystone Venture LLC purchased the business in 2002.

Current owners Mark and Lori Strosahl, with the guidance of the previous owners, have continued the traditions of simple elegance and great food for which the Greystone has become famous. The interior of the restaurant has been restored to be in keeping with the Historic District Preservation Project. The Dining Room offers a more formal setting with crisp linen tablecloths and a formal décor, while the bistro in the front of the building retains the original gray stone walls and tin ceilings. Floral tablecloths topped with glass add to the casual bistro atmosphere, along with Tiffany glass, a beautiful antique backbar, and a 15-foot-long pillared breakfront with marble top and mirrors.

Fresh seafood is delivered daily and the restaurant selects and carves its own beef from large primal cuts, which come from a trusted provider who has proven, over the years, their own commitment to the highest quality. Greystone is a wine-oriented restaurant, as can be observed by the wine list, which offers a large selection of wines by the glass, including about a dozen new wines each month. Many hours are spent in the wine country, developing relationships that enable the restaurant to offer a unique selection.

# PENNE WITH PUMPKIN AND SAUSAGE

We recommend using mild sausage for this recipe, since it is easier to match a wine with milder sausage.

## Ingredients

2 pounds mild or hot Italian sausage

4 tablespoons good olive oil, divided

2 medium yellow or sweet onion, chopped fine

8 garlic cloves, finely chopped

2 cups dry white wine (Select a wine with little or no oak.)

1 bay leaf

4 tablespoons chopped fresh sage or 2 tablespoons dried sage

2 cups fresh pumpkin, roasted & puréed, or canned pure pumpkin

2 cups chicken or dark vegetable stock

1 cup heavy cream

pinch cinnamon

pinch fresh grated nutmeg

cooked penne lisce pasta

fresh ground pepper

fresh parsley, finely chopped

Parmesan cheese, grated

## Preparation

REMOVE sausage from casing and brown in 2 tablespoons of the olive oil over medium-high heat, until almost done through. Remove sausage from pan and drain. In same pan, add the rest of the olive oil and onion and sauté over medium heat for 1 minute. Add garlic and sauté until onion and garlic are just beginning to brown and onions are tender. Add wine to pan and deglaze. Add bay leaf and sage, adding more sage if desired, and reduce liquid by half. Add pumpkin and chicken stock, stirring to blend. Cook over medium heat and let bubble for 2 minutes.

RETURN sausage to pan, add heavy cream, and season with a pinch of cinnamon and fresh grated nutmeg to taste. Simmer to thicken and serve over penne lisce pasta. Garnish with fresh ground pepper, finely chopped parsley, and grated Parmesan cheese.

*Serves 6–8*

# CHICKEN ALMANDINE PESTO
*with Sun-dried Tomato Sauce*

## Ingredients

4   boneless, skinless chicken breasts
8   teaspoons basil pesto
8   teaspoons bacon, cooked till soft crisp
    and chopped
8   teaspoons slivered blanched almonds
8   teaspoons crumbles of Stilton,
    Maytag, Gorgonzola Picante or other
    blue cheese

panko
Sun-dried Tomato Sauce
  (recipe follows)

## Preparation

POUND each chicken breast down to a ¼-inch thickness. Combine basil pesto, bacon crumbles, almonds, and blue cheese crumbles. Divide ingredients into 4 equal portions and roll into chicken breasts. These can be made ahead and refrigerated until ready to cook.

PREHEAT oven to 425 degrees. Roll chicken breasts in panko and place in baking dish. Place in oven for 10 to 15 minutes. Remove from oven and plate with Sun-dried Tomato Sauce over baked chicken.

*Serves 4*

## For the Sun-dried Tomato Sauce

2   cups chicken stock
2   cups heavy cream
¼   cup lemon juice
1   teaspoon garlic powder
5   shots Tabasco® sauce
1   bay leaf

5   whole cloves
¼   cup dry white wine
1   cup sun-dried tomatoes
2   tablespoons white flour
2   tablespoons unsalted butter
    salt & pepper

ADD chicken stock, cream, lemon juice, garlic powder, Tabasco® sauce, bay leaf and cloves to a medium saucepan and heat, stirring occasionally. In a separate pan, sauté sun-dried tomatoes with white wine until soft. Remove from pan and purée in blender. Add back to sauce. Cook a roux with the white flour and butter and add roux to sauce. Bring mixture to a boil to thicken. Strain sauce and keep warm for service.

# Rack of Lamb Greystone

## Ingredients

4   cups chicken stock
2   cups orange juice, preferably fresh
      squeezed
2   cups low sodium soy sauce
1   cup lemon juice
1   cup apple juice
10  garlic cloves, peeled

1   tablespoon whole black peppercorns
1   tablespoon brown sugar
5–7  pounds rack of domestic spring lamb,
      frenched, cap removed and trimmed
      back to loin section
      Basil Chimichurri (recipe follows)

## Preparation

COMBINE all liquids with the garlic, peppercorns, and brown sugar. Marinate trimmed racks in this mixture for 24 hours, and no more than 36 hours, in the refrigerator. Remove from marinade and pat dry. Let meat sit until it reaches room temperature, approximately 30 minutes.

PREHEAT grill to high heat. When ready, grill racks to desired temperature, and serve with Basil Chimichurri.

*Serves 8*

## For the Basil Chimichurri

8   ounces fresh basil, stems removed
8   ounces fresh mint leaves
2   ounces olive oil
4   cloves garlic

1   tablespoon sugar
½   teaspoon salt
dash  Tabasco® sauce

ADD basil and mint to blender or food processor and start processing. While processing, add olive oil, garlic cloves, sugar, and salt. Add a dash of Tabasco sauce. Sauce should be thick, and not run over the plate, when served.

# SYRAH BRAISED BEEF SHORT RIBS

Ask your butcher to cut the short ribs two inches tall, as they will braise better. It is also important to have a brassier of proper size so that most of the rib is out of the liquid braise.

## Ingredients

⅛ cup dried porcini mushrooms
1 1500ml bottle syrah
1 quart veal stock
5–7 pounds 2-inch beef short ribs
1½ yellow onions, coarsely chopped
3 handfuls baby carrots
5 stalks celery, cut into large pieces, with some of the leafy green top
⅛ cup coffee, ground

4 sage leaves
2 sprigs rosemary
4 sprigs thyme leaves
1½ tablespoons green peppercorns
1 tablespoon juniper berries
    salt and cracked black pepper
1 dried whole ancho chile pepper
2 tablespoons unsalted butter

## Preparation

PREHEAT oven to 275 degrees. Place dried porcini mushrooms in a spice blender, grind until fine, and set aside. Place wine and veal stock in a saucepan and reduce by half.

IN oven brassier, brown short ribs on all sides. When ribs are browned, remove them from pan and drain the fat from the pan. Add onions, carrots, and celery and sauté over medium-high heat until onions show a little brown around the edges. Add reduced wine and stock to pan and deglaze. Add coffee, sage, rosemary, thyme, green peppercorns, and juniper berries. Stir briefly. Return short ribs to pan, standing them upright against one another so they do not fall over. Sprinkle the tops of the ribs with the powdered porcini mushrooms, a little salt and cracked black pepper. Add the ancho chile and cover pan.

PLACE pan in 275-degree oven for 2 hours or until the connective tissue is soft and the meat is pulling away from the bones. Remove brassier from oven and remove ribs to a covered holding pan. Strain braising liquid through chinois and de-fat. Reduce liquid over high heat until one quarter remains. Remove sauce from heat and add 2 tablespoons unsalted butter while stirring until sauce acquires a smooth sheen. Serve ribs with sauce and roasted fall vegetables.

*Serves 6*

# Taverna Tagaris

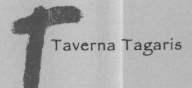

Taverna Tagaris

844 Tulip Lane
Richland, WA 99352
509-628-0020
www.tagariswines.com

Dinner Monday – Thursday
5:00pm – 9:00pm
Friday & Saturday 5:00pm – 10:00pm
Summer Hours for Patio
Monday – Wednesday
11:00am – 9:00pm
Thursday – Saturday
11:00am – 1:00am

# Taverna Tagaris

### Frank Chullino, Chef
### Darren Dewalt, Sous Chef

The unique combination of wineries and fine foods has been a staple in California for decades. Washington State's excellent wineries are beginning to realize the value of that partnership in attracting both tourists and locals alike. Winemaker Michael Taggares is a trailblazer in this aspect. He has been growing grapes since 1983 and founded Tagaris Winery in 1987. The winery honors the proper Greek spelling of the family name, whose members descended from the royal family and first began growing wine grapes in the 15th century.

Tagaris Winery is the modern day result of three generations of grape growers in Washington's Columbia Valley. Michael's grandfather, Pete, left Greece when he was eighteen years old. Grampa Pete made his living in America as a cook on the railroads, crossing the continent by rail. While passing through Prosser, he was moved so strongly by the resemblance of the land to his homeland in Greece that he left the railroad and established a home in Prosser, where he raised a family and began growing apples, grapes, and other crops. He made his own wines and stored them in the family root cellar in wooden casks that now reside in the new Tagaris Winery. Michael's father, Pete, Jr., established himself as the largest farming operation in the State of Washington. Michael followed in his footsteps, presently farming 1,400 acres, 1.5 million Fuji apple trees, and 700 acres of wine grapes in the newly recognized Wahluke AVA.

The taverna—the Greek word for tavern—consists of a spacious wine tasting bar and a large, comfortable restaurant that looks out through floor-to-ceiling windows upon a spacious patio. Patio Kouzina—Greek for kitchen—is a delightful alternative for lunch and dinner during the pleasant summer months. A large grill is used for cooking fresh meat and fish under the open sky. Live music is featured on Friday and Saturday nights in the summer, adding a neighborhood party ambience to the setting.

Fresh and local are the words to describe the cuisine. Local farmers regularly stop by with truckloads of fresh vegetables and fruits, or perhaps a lamb or pig to sell. The cook pulls fresh greens from the side yard or explores the local farmers' market for the best ingredients to enhance the evening's cuisine. And, of course, the Tagaris wines are matched beautifully with the entrées and flatbreads on the menu.

# ROCK SHRIMP & CHORIZO FLATBREAD

This is one of my favorite flatbreads that we make in the Taverna. I believe it is one of the few things on an ever-changing and evolving menu that has been around since the beginning. It seems to appeal to all the senses and the ingredients are easy to get year round. It works well for an appetizer for a few people or even an entrée for one. We make our own dough and chorizo but it is easy enough these days to buy them if you don't have the time.

## Ingredients

- 1 pound Fresh Pizza Dough (recipe follows) or favorite store-bought crust extra virgin olive oil
- 5–7 cloves garlic, chopped fine salt & pepper
- 1 large onion, cut into julienne strips and caramelized
- 1 pound fresh Spanish style chorizo sausage, cooked & chopped

- 1 pound rock shrimp, thawed & peeled
- 2 cups barrel-aged feta cheese, crumbled
- 6 medium-sized tomatoes, roasted, skinned & rough chopped
- 1 bunch green onion, chopped
- 1 bunch fresh cilantro, picked whole leaves

## Preparation

IF using Fresh Pizza Dough, portion into 4 dough balls, cover with a damp towel and let rest for 1 hour in a warm place, and let proof until they have doubled in size.

PREHEAT oven to 475 degrees. Roll out dough to desired size on a floured surface. It can be any shape you want. Spread some extra virgin olive oil on the dough along with some chopped garlic. Season the dough with salt & pepper. Scatter or arrange a quarter of the caramelized onions, chorizo, rock shrimp, feta cheese & chopped tomato around the flatbread evenly. Season again with a little salt & pepper. Repeat process with the other dough balls.

BAKE the flatbreads on a pizza stone or cookie sheets in oven until the dough becomes a deep, crisp golden brown, approximately 20 minutes.

REMOVE flatbread from oven, cut each into 6–8 pieces & garnish with green onions, picked cilantro and a drizzle of extra virgin olive oil.

### Yield: 4 pizzas

*Wine Suggestion: We recommend serving this with a glass of our Kokkino Red Table Wine or our Dry Riesling.*

## For the Fresh Pizza Dough

3½ cups high gluten flour
½ whole wheat flour
2 teaspoons sugar
2 teaspoons kosher salt

¼ ounce fresh yeast
1⅔ cups water, heated to 110°
1 ounce extra virgin olive oil

IN a mixing bowl combine all dry ingredients including yeast. In a counter top mixer with hook attachment, start mixing on medium-low speed, adding water and olive oil. Mix for 6–8 minutes. Do not over mix or dough will be tough. The dough will come together and be moist and the bowl will be clean. Let dough proof at room temperature until it doubles in size.

THIS dough is great for foccacia, as well as pizza. After dough has proofed, you can form dough balls for pizza—for foccacia, form it to fit a cookie sheet. Let the dough proof again to the size you want, top it with your favorites and bake away.

---

# Washington Cherry Gazpacho
### with Curried Yogurt, Toasted Almonds & Cilantro

Here is a fun twist on a classic Spanish gazpacho. This is a recipe for the late spring and early summer, when Eastern Washington is starting to really heat up and the local cherries seem to be everywhere. In this recipe we also like to call on a local favorite, the Walla Walla sweet onion and some of the other bountiful neighborhood crops. The curried yogurt is a cool addition when popped into an ice cream machine and turned into a frozen yogurt. If you don't have an ice cream maker, a drizzle of yogurt will work just fine. We prefer black cherries, which give an impressive presentation, especially with the contrast of the yogurt and the cilantro.

## Ingredients

2 pounds black cherries, pitted
1 large Walla Walla sweet onion, peeled & sliced
1 large cucumber, peeled & seeded
2 cups bread, crusts removed, soaked in cold water & drained
8–10 fresh garlic cloves
3 Serrano chiles, sliced & stem removed

½ cup verjus rouge
½ cup Cabernet vinegar or cider vinegar
2 cups extra virgin olive oil
salt & pepper – to taste
juice of 1 lemon, to taste
Curried Yogurt (recipe follows)
¼ cup toasted almonds, chopped
fresh cilantro leaves, picked from stem

## Preparation

COMBINE cherries, onion, cucumber, bread, garlic, chilies, verjus, and vinegar in a food processor. Blend, adding olive oil through the top until smooth. Add salt, pepper, and lemon juice to taste. Place in a bowl or container and refrigerate until needed. It can keep overnight.

TO SERVE, ladle gazpacho into serving bowls. Drizzle Curried Yogurt over or around the gazpacho and sprinkle with toasted almonds and cilantro leaves.

*Serves 4 to 6*

*Wine Suggestion: Serve as a soup course on a hot day with a glass of Sangria.*

## For the Curried Yogurt

| | |
|---|---|
| 1 cup plain yogurt | lemon juice – to taste |
| ¼ cup honey | salt & pepper – to taste |
| 2 tablespoons yellow curry powder (Madras, Poudre de Colombo, etc) | |

IN A mixing bowl combine yogurt, honey, and curry powder and mix thoroughly. Season with lemon juice, salt, and pepper to taste. Refrigerate until needed. It can keep for a few days.

*Rock Shrimp & Chorizo Flatbread*

# GOAT CHEESE TORTELLI

*with Orange Kabocha Squash Agrodolce, Brown Butter and Sage*

Fall happens to be one of my favorite seasons. One can never go wrong with this timeless combination. Now more than ever this would be my favorite twist on the old classic. The squash from our friends at Wild Iris Farms down the street, the goat cheese from our friends at Monteillet Fromagerie, the local sage... I even like to sneak in a little fresh-squeezed grape juice just in from harvest and fresh out of the press. If you can't find kabocha squash, butternut squash is a great substitute. Just be sure to take the skin off it. I like the orange kabocha because you can eat the skin with its beautiful fall color. Don't be intimidated by making fresh pasta. It is not as hard as you would think, and the rewards are great.

## Ingredients

1 pound butter, divided
1 melon-sized orange kabocha squash, skin on, seeded, medium dice
½ cup maple syrup
1 cinnamon stick
½ cup cider vinegar
2 cups white grape juice, if available salt & pepper to taste
1 cup amaretti cookies, or similar almond cookie, divided

1 cup fresh Parmesan cheese, grated, plus extra for garnish
1 fresh nutmeg, to be grated
Fresh Pasta Dough (recipe follows)
Goat Cheese Filling (recipe follows)
semolina flour
1 bunch fresh sage, picked and cut into thin strips

## Preparation

HEAT a large sauté pan or non-reactive pot on medium high. Add about a tablespoon of the butter to the pan and let it melt. Add diced squash and maple syrup and cook for a couple minutes, stirring regularly. Add cinnamon stick, vinegar, and grape juice. Simmer until squash is tender and then season with salt and pepper to taste.

PLACE ⅓ of this mixture in a food processor and add the amaretti cookies, reserving 4 cookies to be crumbled for garnish. Add the cup of grated Parmesan cheese and a little fresh grated nutmeg. Purée until smooth and reserve.

DIVIDE Fresh Pasta Dough into 2 pieces. Put the dough through a pasta machine, folding into halves each time, and then reinserting 15–20 times, to knead it. Continue until the pasta is paper-thin. Lay out the sheets of dough and cut them into 4-inch squares.

PLACE 1 heaping tablespoon of Goat Cheese Filling on one corner of each square. Fold over the filled portion, press down around the filling, and place on a baking sheet lined with wax paper and sprinkle with semolina.

MAKE the brown butter by melting the remaining butter in a large skillet over medium-high heat and cook until it begins to foam and brown, about 4 minutes. Add sage, squash purée, diced squash mix, and salt and pepper to taste. You could add about ½ cup of the pasta water to thin out sauce, if desired.

BRING a large pot of water—salted, if desired—to a boil over high heat. Add the filled pasta and cook until they are tender, about 3 minutes. Toss with the brown butter and squash mixture and serve immediately, garnishing with grated Parmesan and the reserved crumbled amaretti cookies.

*Serves 4–6*

*Wine Suggestion: This recipe makes for a great fall pasta course, or just a meal in itself with a nice glass of dry Riesling or Pino Gris.*

## For the Fresh Pasta Dough

| | |
|---|---|
| 2–2½ cups all-purpose flour | 2 large eggs |
| 1 teaspoon kosher salt | 3 large egg yolks |

COMBINE all ingredients into a countertop mixer with a dough hook. Mix on low until everything is incorporated. You should have firm yet elastic dough. Cover with plastic wrap and let rest while you prepare the squash and filling.

## For the Goat Cheese Filling

| | |
|---|---|
| ¾ pound fresh goat cheese | ¼ pound fresh ricotta cheese |
| ¼ teaspoons fresh grated nutmeg | salt & pepper to taste |

COMBINE the ingredients and season to taste with salt & pepper. Refrigerate until ready to make the pasta.

# King Salmon in Tagine
*with Honey Roasted Baby Onions, Peaches, Pluots, Grapes, & Cilantro Couscous*

This is a Moroccan-inspired dish that we think showcases the abundant summertime fruit here in Eastern Washington. You can get creative, if you like, by substituting cherries, plums, any of your summertime favorites. Using different types of baby onions is fun, too. We use candy and red onions grown by one of our favorite farm girls at Hanson Farms in Pasco. Tagines are a conical cooking vessel that is traditional to Moroccan cooking. It is used to incorporate all the flavors of a dish and keep the food moist and delicious. If you don't have a tagine, you can use a cast iron pan with a lid for a somewhat similar effect.

## Ingredients

¼ cup honey
1 pound baby onions (red or candy sweet) peeled
2 pounds fresh king salmon fillet, cut into 4 pieces
olive oil
2–3 cloves fresh garlic, peeled & chopped
2–3 shallots, peeled and sliced thin
1 thumb-sized nugget of ginger root, peeled & fine diced, divided
1 cup verjus

1 cup white grape juice
1 pound seedless grapes, stemmed & washed
2–3 whole peaches, pitted & sliced
2–3 whole pluots, pitted & sliced
½ cup toasted almonds (chopped or slivered) for garnish
⅓ bunch fresh cilantro, picked, for garnish
Cilantro Couscous (recipe follows)

## Preparation

COMBINE honey and baby onions and roast in 425-degree oven until tender. Keep warm for service.

HEAT a large tagine bottom on medium-high on the stovetop. Add a capful of olive oil and sauté garlic and shallots until just golden. Add half of the ginger along with the verjus and reduce by half. Add grape juice and simmer for 5 minutes. Add grapes, peaches, pluots.

PLACE salmon on fruit and simmer, covered, on stovetop until salmon is cooked to desired temperature. Medium is recommended, about 5–7 minutes.

REMOVE from heat and serve in tagine garnished with toasted almonds and fresh picked cilantro, with roasted baby onions and Cilantro Couscous on the side.

### Serves 4

*Wine Suggestion: We recommend this dish with our White Meritage or Gewürztraminer.*

## For the Cilantro Couscous

*1 box couscous (cooked according to the box instructions)*
*⅔ bunch cilantro, picked*
*1 whole Serrano chile, stemmed & chopped*

*2 fresh garlic cloves*
*1 bunch green onions, ends trimmed and chopped*
*extra virgin olive oil*
*lemon juice*

COMBINE picked cilantro, Serrano chile, garlic, and onion, and purée in blender or food processor, slowly adding enough olive oil to get a nice purée consistency. Prepare couscous according to instructions. When done, add cilantro purée to couscous and serve with tagine.

# CARAMEL APPLE FLATBREAD
### with Vanilla Bean Ice Cream, Spiced Apple Compote, & Caramel Sauce

If you love apple pie this flatbread is for you. This flatbread has worked its way into being one of the staples here at Taverna Tagaris and has an interesting story as to its origins. It so happens I asked owner, Mike Taggares, for some apples one day, since he has apple orchards too. Mike started bringing us apples and before I knew it I had more apples than thought I would or could ever know what to do with. We made a bunch of apple compote, some home-made vanilla ice cream, and a little caramel with streusel topping, put it on our flatbread and next thing you knew we had a winner. This is a great dessert to share with a group.

## Ingredients

¼  cup brown sugar
½  cup cider vinegar
 5  apples, medium dice
¼  cup cinnamon
    lemon juice to taste
    Fresh Pizza Dough (see recipe in this section)

Streusel Topping (recipe follows)
good quality vanilla ice cream
Caramel Sauce (recipe follows)
confectionary sugar and fresh basil, for garnish

## Preparation

COMBINE brown sugar and cider vinegar and bring to a boil in saucepot. Add apples, cinnamon, and a little lemon juice to taste. Cook until soft, stirring regularly, for about 20 minutes. Let cool and reserve compote for later.

PREHEAT oven to 500 degrees with a baking stone. (You can use a cookie sheet if you don't have a stone.) Dust countertop lightly with flour, and roll out dough to desired size—it should be thin. Place on floured cutting pizza paddle or small cutting board and distribute apple compote over flatbread dough in a thin layer. Sprinkle Streusel Topping over compote. Slide flatbread onto preheated baking stone and cook for approximately 10 minutes, or until the dough is crisp throughout and a deep golden brown.

REMOVE from oven and place vanilla ice cream randomly on the flatbread. Cut into desired amount of pieces and drizzle Caramel Sauce over flatbread. Sprinkle with confectionery sugar and garnish with fresh basil. Enjoy!

### Serves 6

*Wine Suggestion: Serve with a nice late harvest white wine.*

## For the Streusel Topping

6 ounces light brown sugar
6 ounces granulated sugar
11 ounces butter
1 tablespoon ground cinnamon

2 teaspoons salt
1 teaspoon vanilla extract
1 pound bread flour

COMBINE all ingredients and mix until crumbly.

## For the Caramel Sauce

2 cups brown sugar
¼ pound butter

½ vanilla bean
1 cup heavy cream

MELT butter over medium-high heat, add sugar and stir. Cook for couple minutes then stir in the heavy cream. Add vanilla and let cool. Should be a syrupy consistency at room temperature.

# SAFFRON & RIESLING POACHED PEAR

*with Honeycomb and Vanilla Mascarpone*

## Ingredients

1 bottle Riesling
2 whole cinnamon sticks
1 cup honey
1 pinch saffron
4 large ripe pears

1 pint mascarpone
1 vanilla bean or 1 tablespoon vanilla
   extract
honeycomb, broken in pieces
basil sprigs for garnish

## Preparation

IN A pot large enough to hold the pears submerged, combine Riesling, cinnamon, honey and saffron. Peel pears and place in poaching liquid. Be sure the poaching liquid covers the pears. Bring to a simmer and cook until tender, or when you can push a knife through with no resistance, about 20–25 minutes. Remove from heat and let pears cool in liquid.

WHEN pears are cool, remove them from the liquid and set aside. Heat the poaching liquid on medium-high heat and reduce until a syrupy consistency is achieved. Remove from heat and let cool.

COMBINE mascarpone and vanilla and keep chilled.

TO SERVE, spoon the saffron Riesling syrup into the middle of the serving platter. Place pears on syrup. Arrange honeycomb pieces among the pears. Place dollops of vanilla mascarpone among the pears and honeycomb, and garnish with basil sprigs.

*Serves 4*

# Whitehouse-Crawford Restaurant

## Jamie Guerin, Chef

The growth of wineries in the Walla Walla valley has been spectacular in recent years. From a total of five wineries in the area in 1990, the region now has over sixty. As the wineries have increased, so has the number of sophisticated dining establishments in this sleepy little southeastern Washington town. Walla Walla has always had a special small town, comfortable ambiance. It is the home of the nationally esteemed liberal arts college, Whitman College, with its famous alumnus, Supreme Court Justice William O. Douglas.

In 2000, the Whitehouse-Crawford Restaurant opened its doors to treat residents and visitors alike to a fine dining establishment and a chance to immerse them in a special piece of Walla Walla's history. The restaurant is housed in an old lumber planing mill and furniture factory. The original wood structure on the site dates back to 1880, but was destroyed by fire in 1903. The mill was rebuilt of brick and completed in October 1904. The mill operated until its sale to the City of Walla Walla in 1988. The city planned to sell the building as part of a larger land acquisition for development of a 4-story motel. However, the public protest eventually stopped the transaction, and the building was acquired and lovingly restored by its current owner, appropriately named Salvation! LLC. It is now listed on the Washington Heritage Register and the National Register of Historic Places.

The interior of the restaurant is a delight. The airy high ceilings and the magnificent red fir floor are set off by crisp white tablecloths and bright blue upholstered chairs. Seven Hills Winery shares part of the building, and offers a unique view of its barrel room. Diners in the restaurant can view the enormous oak casks stacked to the rafters through a floor-to-ceiling paned windows. The walls are decorated with many historic photos of the mill workers and their children, and the entrance displays the original iron boiler door.

To preside over the kitchen the owners, Sonia and Carl Schmitt, brought in celebrated chef, Jamie Guerin, from Seattle's prestigious restaurant, Campagne. When asked to describe the cuisine at Whitehouse-Crawford, Jamie answers, "It is mostly made up of all the things I like." Jamie has created a menu that changes daily, and is largely composed of locally grown and raised produce and meats. By the entrance to the restaurant hangs a framed letter from Alice Waters, thanking Jamie for an enjoyable meal and inviting him to Chez Panisse. What better tribute can a chef receive?

# Walla Walla Sweet Onion Sambal

This goes well with grilled poultry or fish, or with bread or crackers as an hors d'oeuvre. My Sri Lankan pastry chef, Nimal, taught me how to make this. Onion sambal is usually served at room temperature or chilled.

## Ingredients

7 Walla Walla onions, diced
   vegetable oil
3 cinnamon sticks
1½ teaspoons whole cardamom
¾ teaspoon whole cloves
¾ teaspoon red chili flakes

4 tablespoons sugar
½ cup white wine vinegar
1 teaspoon ground black pepper
3 ounces tamarind paste, steeped in 1
   cup of hot water
   salt to taste

## Preparation

IN A large, wide pan heat vegetable oil over high heat and add onions. Add cinnamon sticks and sauté the onions until they begin to caramelize. Grind the cardamom and cloves together in a spice grinder. Add spices to onions along with chili flakes, sugar, vinegar, and pepper. Turn down heat and let onions soften.

SQUEEZE the tamarind paste and the water with your hands to form a paste and pass this through a strainer to remove seeds. Add this paste to the onions and allow onions to cook a little longer. Season to taste with salt. Before serving, let mixture cool to room temperature or chill, whichever temperature is desired.

*Yield: about 3 cups*

# BUTTERNUT SQUASH SOUP
### with Thai Curry and Coconut Milk

This soup is easy to make and the Thai flavors add a definite kick. It is very satisfying on a chilly fall day.

## Ingredients

1 onion, peeled & sliced
1 carrot, peeled & sliced
1 1-inch piece fresh ginger, peeled & grated
4 tablespoons butter
1 quart coconut milk

2 cups vegetable or chicken stock
1 butternut squash, peeled, seeded, & cut into chunks
1 tablespoon Thai yellow curry paste
1 tablespoon Thai fish sauce
salt to taste

## Preparation

SLOWLY cook onion, carrot, and ginger in butter until soft. Add coconut milk, stock, and squash and bring to a simmer. Add curry paste and fish sauce and simmer until all the vegetables are very soft.

IN A food processor or blender, blend soup in batches, adding more stock, if necessary, to achieve the right consistency. Season to taste with salt.

### Yield: about 2 quarts

# SPINACH SOUP WITH FRESH CILANTRO

We get beautiful, locally grown spinach in Walla Walla and make this simple, yet very comforting soup. The bright green color is very appetizing.

## Ingredients

| | |
|---|---|
| 1 small onion, sliced | 1½ quarts chicken or vegetable stock |
| 1 leek, sliced | 1 cup white wine |
| 2 cloves garlic, chopped | 1 pound fresh spinach, washed |
| 1 medium potato, peeled and cut into chunks | ½ bunch fresh cilantro, leaves only |
| butter | salt & pepper to taste |
| | toasted pine nuts, for garnish |

## Preparation

SLOWLY cook onion, leek, garlic, and potato in a little butter until soft and without any color. Add stock and wine and let simmer until flavor develops. Add spinach and cilantro and simmer until spinach turns bright green. Place soup in a blender and blend until smooth.

IMMEDIATELY cool the soup by pouring it into a bowl that is on top of another bowl that is filled with ice. This will help the soup keep its color. If you are going to eat the soup right away, you can skip this step. Season soup with salt and pepper and garnish with toasted pine nuts.

*Yield: 1½ quarts*

SHOW-CASES
FURNITURE AND STORE FIXTURES.
WHITEHOUSE-CRAWFORD CO
PLANING MILL.

1904 - 2004

# SESAME-CILANTRO PESTO

I remember my first chef in Santa Fe making this sauce to go with salmon. It goes well with chicken, fish, or on vegetables. We've received many requests for this recipe.

## Ingredients

2 bunches cilantro, washed, big stems removed
1 avocado, peeled and pit removed
2 cloves garlic, peeled
1 small jalapeño, stem removed

3 tablespoons roasted sesame tahini
2 tablespoons fresh lime juice
2 tablespoons honey
1 cup mild tasting olive oil
salt to taste

## Preparation

PLACE all ingredients, except the oil and salt, in a blender. Turn on blender and slowly add the olive oil to achieve a bright green paste. Add more oil if too thick. Season to taste with salt.

*Yield: 2 cups*

---

# HUCKLEBERRY CRÊPES
### with Mascarpone Cream

Local huckleberries are easily found in the Blue Mountains, just east of Walla Walla, and I have enjoyed using them in many of my desserts. These light, delicate crêpes highlight this exotic berry and can be enjoyed during late summer at our restaurant.

## Ingredients

1 pound huckleberries
1 cup sugar
2 tablespoons lemon juice
20 Crêpes (recipe follows)

Mascarpone Cream (recipe follows)
grated orange zest, for garnish
huckleberries tossed in granulated sugar, for garnish

## Preparation

IN A saucepan combine huckleberries, sugar, and lemon juice and cook over medium heat for 5–7 minutes. Strain the juice back into a saucepan. Save the strained huckleberries—that is now the compote—and chill in refrigerator. Reduce the juice to a third over low heat. Cool the huckleberry sauce in the refrigerator. When compote is needed, add 2 tablespoons of the huckleberry sauce to coat the huckleberry compote.

PREHEAT oven to 350 degrees. Reheat 2 crêpes, per serving, in oven for about 2 minutes. Fold crêpes into quarters. Lift top flap and fill each crêpe with 1 heaping tablespoon of Mascarpone Cream. Place crêpes on a plate. Place 1 tablespoon of the huckleberry compote at the opening of each crêpe. Drizzle about 2 teaspoons of huckleberry sauce around the bottom of the crêpes. Garnish with sugar coated huckleberries and grated orange zest.

*Serves 10*

## For the Crêpes

|  |  |
|---|---|
| 2 cups milk | 1 tablespoon vegetable oil |
| ¼ teaspoon salt | 3 whole eggs |
| 7 tablespoons sugar | 2 tablespoons vanilla extract |
| 4 tablespoons butter | 2 tablespoons cherry liqueur |
| 1¼ cups all-purpose flour | ½ cup beer |

HEAT the milk, salt, sugar, and butter in a saucepan over medium heat until butter is melted. In a bowl mix flour, vegetable oil, eggs, vanilla extract, and cherry liqueur. In a blender combine the milk mixture and the flour mixture until smooth. Strain the crêpe batter into a container. Add the beer and mix by hand just to incorporate. Cover and chill in the refrigerator for at least 2 hours.

HEAT a small crêpe pan (or small fry pan) over medium heat. Using a paper towel to apply vegetable oil, lightly coat the pan. Place about 3 tablespoons of batter in to the middle of the pan and swirl around until it evenly coats the pan. Cook until batter on top starts to dry out and the edges are slightly brown, about 1½ minutes. Use a spatula (or pallet knife) to turn the crêpe over. Cook about 1 more minute. Remove to a cooling rack until cooled off.

## For the Mascarpone Cream

|  |  |
|---|---|
| 1 cup whipping cream | 1 tablespoon cherry liqueur |
| 6 tablespoons powdered sugar | 1 tablespoon vanilla extract |
| ½ pound mascarpone cream | |

PLACE whipping cream and sugar in a mixing bowl and beat on medium speed, just to soft peak. Add mascarpone and mix on medium speed until medium peak. Add cherry liqueur and vanilla extract and mix by hand. Do not over mix. Keep in refrigerator until needed.

*Photographer Lawrence Denny Lindsley was the grandson of Seattle pioneers David T. and Louisa Boren Denny. He bought his first camera through a magazine subscription, and got his start as a scenic photographer with the firm of W.P. Romans in 1890. Lindsley started his own business in 1919. He is particularly known for his photographs of the Lake Chelan, Grand Coulee, and Mount Rainier areas.*

# Whoopemup Hollow Café

120 Main Street    Dinner
Waitsburg, WA    Tuesday – Sunday
509-337-9000    3:00pm – 9:00pm

# Whoopemup Hollow Café

**Bryant Bader, Chef/Owner**
**Valerie Mudry, Pastry Chef/Owner**
**Ross Stevenson, Dining Room Manager/Owner**
**Leroy Cunningham, Designer/Owner**

Just a short twenty miles east of Walla Walla sits the quaint little town of Waitsburg. The town is surrounded by the rolling hills of the Palouse region, which is famous for the wheat, peas, and barley grown in its rich soil. The area gives off a laid back, comfortable ambiance that harkens back to days gone by. There is a sense of community and inclusion that draws the visitor in.

Four friends, who came to the area to enjoy each other's company, were drawn in by this special feeling and began to collaborate on a project that would involve them all—the Whoopemup Hollow Café. Named for one of Waitsburg's local hollows, the café opened in May 2005, with each member of the group contributing his or her special talents to the project.

Bryant Bader was born in Brainerd, Minnesota, beside the headwaters of the Mississippi River. With over 25 years experience in the kitchens of the Seattle culinary scene, Bryant brings a sense of magic to cooking, often going on instinct and what's literally at hand. Valerie Mudry also has about 25 years experience in the Seattle restaurant scene, including a seven-year stint at Campagne. Most recently, she worked at Todd English's Fish Club Restaurant at the Seattle Marriott. Her creations always have people reaching for their cameras—and they taste even better! She also is a chocolatier, which means lovely chocolate truffles for the restaurant.

Ross Stevenson, the Dining Room Manager, describes himself as, "Jack of all trades, master of???" He also has a total of 25 years experience in both the front and back of the house, working at such notable Seattle restaurants Café Campagne and Flying Fish, before moving to Waitsburg in 2000. Designer, Leroy Cunningham, has utilized his carpentry talents in creating a comfortable dining space to match the comfort of the food. With maple and birch, and warm colors, the interior is a testament to his creativity. The dining room is lined with spacious booths, all individually milled and custom built.

Although none in the group is truly "Southern," they have created an atmosphere of Southern hospitality, featuring Southern comfort foods. They embrace all regional Southern cuisines, be it Cajun, Creole, Carolina Low Country, of the Cubano influence in Florida. Focusing on fresh, seasonal ingredients, they prepare almost everything from scratch, including their own hamburger buns.

# SAVORY CORN FRITTERS

After searching for a good corn fritter recipe, I just made one up and here it is in its current state of evolution. The freeze-dried corn is a great product. I can usually find it in the produce department of the grocery store. Melissa's is the most common brand. If you can't find candied jalapeños, substitute with canned or fresh and add a bit of maple syrup.

## Ingredients

½ cup leeks, chopped (white part only)
1 tablespoon shallots, chopped
2 tablespoons garlic, chopped
1 tablespoon butter
1 tablespoon salt
1 tablespoon lemon pepper
¼ cup sherry
½ cup green onions, chopped
½ cup candied jalapeños

½ cup red pepper, chopped
2 cups corn (fresh or frozen)
2 eggs
1 cup cream
½ cup freeze-dried corn, ground in food processor
2 cups cake flour
oil for frying (I use canola)

## Preparation

SAUTÉ leeks, shallots, and garlic in butter. Add salt and lemon pepper. Add sherry and reduce until liquid is almost gone. Cool. Add green onions, jalapeños, red pepper, and corn to this mixture and set aside. In a large bowl, whisk eggs and cream together, then add the ground freeze-dried corn. Fold in vegetable mixture. Slowly mix in the cake flour until it's just incorporated. Set aside.

POUR oil into large heavy-duty pot to about 3 inches in depth—if you have a little deep fryer, even better. Heat oil to 325 degrees. Shape the dough with 2 spoons and carefully drop the fritters into the hot oil. Cook for 4 or 5 minutes, until colored to a nice golden brown. Remove from oil and place on a rack to cool

*Serves 8*

# QUICK SOUTHERN GREENS

Traditionally, Southern greens can be an all-day affair because they use "meatier" greens such as collard and mustard that take a long time to cook. I've made this recipe for home cooks who may not have the time or patience for traditional southern greens.

There are so many greens from which to choose. I love chard and escarole together. They cook quickly, but also can handle longer cooking times.

## Ingredients

1 large bunch chard (rainbow chard is my favorite, but red and swiss are fine)
large head escarole
½ red onion, julienne
½ red pepper, julienne
2 tablespoons garlic, minced
3 tablespoons olive oil or bacon fat

1 tablespoon salt
½ tablespoon black pepper
1 tablespoon thyme
½ tablespoon paprika
2 ounces sherry
1 ounce balsamic vinegar
4 ounces tomato sauce

## Preparation

WASH the greens, removing the stems from the chard. Coarsely chop and set aside. In a large skillet sauté onions, peppers, and garlic in oil/fat of your choice. Season with salt, pepper, thyme, and paprika. Add the sherry, then the vinegar and tomato sauce. Simmer for 1–2 minutes, and then add the greens, turning them until they begin to cook down. Cover and set aside until ready to serve.

*Serves 6–8*

---

# BLACKBERRY CHIPOTLE BARBEQUE RIBS

Originally, I started out using raspberries, but found the flavor of blackberries to be deeper and richer and have used them ever since. I also use a special ingredient in this recipe—Cajun Power® Garlic Sauce. Often available in grocery stores, it can be ordered online at www.cajunpowersauce.com. They have many great products and I actually use their chipotle jelly instead of the preserves in the BBQ sauce.

## Ingredients

1 side baby back pork ribs, to serve 2-3 people

BBQ Dry Rub (recipe follows)
Blackberry Chipotle BBQ Sauce

## Preparation

RUB the ribs with a BBQ Dry Rub. You can also use a commercial rub or make your own. I've included a recipe for a simple one, but feel free to experiment and get carried away. Cover and let sit overnight.

FIRE up your grill or smoker to a low temp and place ribs on grill and cook until outsides are browned. Remove from grill and brush with Blackberry Chipotle BBQ Sauce.

PREHEAT oven to 350 degrees. Place ribs in a baking dish with a little water in the pan. Cover and bake about 40 minutes. Remove and slather with more sauce and serve. Don't forget lots of napkins!

### Yield: 1 side for every 2–3 people served

*Wine Suggestion: We recommend a hearty red wine, such as Forgeron Cellars Zinfandel.*

## For the BBQ Dry Rub

½  cup sea salt
¼  cup brown sugar
2  tablespoons black pepper
2  tablespoons paprika (use smoked paprika if you don't have a smoker)

1  tablespoon celery seed
2  tablespoons chili powder
   fennel seed, cumin or coriander are other nice additions

COMBINE all ingredients well and use as desired.

## For the Blackberry Chipotle BBQ Sauce

2  tablespoons oil (olive or canola)
2  medium onions, coarsely chopped
2  red peppers, coarsely chopped
¼  cup garlic, chopped
1½  cups red wine
1½  cups apple cider vinegar
2  pounds blackberries (fresh or frozen), seeds removed with sieve or food mill
1  12-ounce jar blackberry preserves

2  16-ounce cans tomato purée
1  8-ounce bottle Cajun Power® garlic sauce
1  6-ounce can chipotle peppers in adobo sauce (use less if you want to cut back on heat)
2  tablespoons brown sugar
¼  cup balsamic vinegar
   salt and pepper to taste

HEAT oil in large saucepan. Add onions, peppers and garlic and sauté until translucent. Add red wine and apple cider vinegar. Bring to a simmer and slowly reduce liquid to one half. Add the rest of the ingredients and simmer for 15 minutes, stirring occasionally. Let cool, transfer to food processor and blend until smooth.

### Yield: about 1 ½ quarts

# RED VELVET CAKE
## with Double Cream Cheese Frosting

The origins of red velvet cake are unknown and make fodder for urban legend. We serve it during the summer months at the Whoopemup with strawberry compote.

## Ingredients

vegetable spray, for preparing cake pans

2 tablespoons cocoa powder, for dusting cake pans

2 cups granulated sugar

2½ cups all-purpose flour

¼ cup low fat cocoa powder, such as Hershey's or Ambrosia (do not use Dutch processed cocoa)

1 teaspoon ground cinnamon

1¾ teaspoons baking soda

1 teaspoon baking powder

3 whole eggs

1 cup hot water

2 tablespoons red food coloring

2 tablespoons vinegar

1 cup buttermilk

2 teaspoons real vanilla extract

½ cup (2 sticks) unsalted butter, melted

Double Cream Cheese Frosting (recipe follows)

toasted crushed pecans or chocolate shavings, for garnish

## Preparation

PREHEAT oven to 350 degrees. Prepare two 9-inch cake pans with vegetable pan spray and dust with cocoa powder, making sure to tap out any excess cocoa powder. Sift all dry ingredients together into a large mixing bowl or bowl of stand mixer. Use paddle attachment of stand mixer or hand mix to thoroughly combine ingredients.

MIX together the hot water, food coloring and vinegar. Whisk eggs, colored water mixture, buttermilk, and vanilla extract together in medium-size bowl. Pour wet mixture and melted unsalted butter into dry mixture. Mix cake batter until smooth, scraping down sides of bowl to make sure all ingredients are well mixed. Pour batter into prepared pans as evenly as possible. Tap the pans on the counter top to settle any air bubbles. This will improve the cake's texture. Place in preheated oven and bake for 15–20 minutes. When done, the center of the cake will spring back when pressed and a toothpick, when inserted, will come out clean. Turn cakes out of pans onto wire cooling racks and allow to cool completely before frosting.

WHEN cool, frost the top of one cake approximately ¼-inch thick. Top with the remaining round of cake, then frost sides and top. There should be plenty of frosting left to pipe decorations on cake top and sides if you wish. Be creative! You can decorate the cake sides with toasted crushed pecans or chocolate shavings. Cut in to 8–12 servings while cake is chilled, but serve the cake at room temperature.

*Whoopemup Hollow Café*

**Serves 8–12**

## For the Double Cream Cheese Frosting

½  pound cream cheese, softened
¼  pound (1 stick) unsalted butter,
    softened
1  cup sifted confectioner's sugar

1  teaspoon real vanilla extract
1  teaspoon fresh lemon juice (optional)
¼  cup mascarpone, at room temperature

USING a stand mixer or large mixing bowl with hand mixer with paddle attachment, mix cream cheese, soft butter, and sifted sugar until light and creamy. Add vanilla and lemon juice. Mix thoroughly. Add softened mascarpone and mix gently; do not over mix or mascarpone will become grainy in texture.

*The San Juan Islands were a favorite place for hunting and fishing trips. In this photo, taken in the San Juans, two men cook a meal on an old circular saw blade set above a campfire. One man sits waiting, and another stands with his rifle. Fishing gear, wading boots, and crates of supplies lie nearby. Webster & Stevens took a series of photographs of camping, fishing, and hunting in the San Juan Islands sometime between 1902 and 1910. [between 1902 and 1910]*

# Weinhard Café

**Weinhard Café**

258 East Main Street
Dayton, WA 99328
509-382-1681
www.weinhard-café.com

Lunch
Tuesday – Saturday from 11:00am
Dinner
Tuesday – Saturday from 5:00pm

# Weinhard Café

### Tiffany Cain, Chef/Owner
### Mae Schrey, Chef/Owner

The bucolic town of Dayton is rich in history. The area was originally explored by Lewis and Clark, who camped on Patit Creek just east of Dayton on their return in 1806. At that time, Dayton's main street was a racetrack for regional Indian tribes. The first settlers arrived in 1859, first as ranchers and then as farmers due to the highly fertile soil and adequate rainfall in the area. In 1880, Jacob Weinhard came to town. He was a German immigrant who had first spent time in Portland, where he worked as a foreman at his Uncle Henry's brewery. The rich soil of the area was perfect for growing barley, and Jacob soon established the Jacob Weinhard brewery in Dayton. In 1890, he constructed the Weinhard Hotel building to house the Weinhard Saloon and the Weinhard Lodge.

The Weinhard Café originally was housed on the ground floor of the Weinhard Hotel but, in January 2004, the owners moved the café across the street from the hotel, retaining the Weinhard name. The building they are currently in also has historic value. It originally housed Wm. Chandler's meat market. An old photograph of the meat market's original proprietors hangs on the wall of the café today, showing them posing in front of the building in their butcher's attire. The café's owners have created a delightful turn on this old photo by posing in a similar fashion on the steps of the entrance in their culinary attire.

Tiffany Cain and Mae Schrey have put together a menu that they describe as "eclectic new American cuisine. The ladies are committed to using local produce in their kitchen. Organic produce is supplied by Wild Bill, the gardener, My Grandmother's Garden supplies the café with edible flowers, sweet corn, peppers, and Yukon Gold potatoes. The cheese comes from Monteillet Fromagerie, an organic sheep and goat dairy run by Joan and Pierre-Louis Monteillet in Dayton. The Dayton Farmer's Market is also utilized for fresh herbs, wax beans, and purple potatoes.

The two chefs work side-by-side in the kitchen, with Mae specializing in the mouth-watering baked goods. Mae also selects the wines, and presents her favorites on a chalkboard. The full wine list features the best of the Northwest wines and a beer list offers a good selection of microbrews. The café is a casual and comfortable affair, where exceptional food is served and a friendly, small town atmosphere pervades.

# PEAR SALAD
*with Cider Vinaigrette and Fried Goat Cheese*

## Ingredients

4 rounds fresh goat cheese, each about
  2½ inches in diameter and ½ inch
  thick
½ cup fresh bread crumbs seasoned with
  salt and pepper

vegetable oil for frying
4 cups mixed salad greens, cleaned
  Cider Vinaigrette (recipe follows)
2 Bosc pears, cored and sliced
3 tablespoons toasted pecans

## Preparation

PRESS the cheese rounds into the breadcrumb mixture. Heat a frying pan with vegetable oil. Fry the rounds until golden on each side. Toss the greens with the Cider Vinaigrette and divide among four plates. Top with the sliced pears, toasted nuts, and fried cheese.

*Serves 4*

## For the Cider Vinaigrette

1 cup apple cider
½ cup apple cider vinegar
1 cup olive oil

salt and pepper to taste
1 teaspoon Dijon mustard

PUT cider and vinegar in a small saucepan. Boil until reduced by half. Cool. Whisk in the olive oil and salt , pepper, and mustard.

# Pan Seared Scallops
## with Roasted Pepper Coulis and Black Olive Risotto Cakes

## Ingredients

16 large sea scallops, side muscles
   removed
   kosher salt and black pepper
3 tablespoons unsalted butter

Black Olive Risotto Cakes
   (recipe follows)
Roasted Pepper Coulis (recipe follows)
chopped fresh parsley, for garnish

## Preparation

SPRINKLE scallops with salt and pepper. Melt the butter in a very large skillet over medium-high heat. Cook butter until beginning to brown, and sear scallops, about 2 minutes per side.

TO SERVE, place Black Olive Risotto Cakes on plates and dollop each risotto cake with some Roasted Pepper Coulis and add the seared scallops. Garnish with chopped fresh parsley.

### Serves 4

*Wine Suggestion: A nice, crisp Riesling would pair well with this.*

## For the Black Olive Risotto Cakes

8 cups chicken stock, homemade or
   good quality canned
2 tablespoons butter
1 medium onion, diced
2 cups Arborio rice
½ cup dry white wine

½ cup pecorino cheese
½ cup Nicoise olives, chopped and pitted
2 tablespoons fresh thyme, finely
   chopped
1 egg, lightly beaten
2 tablespoons vegetable oil

PLACE the stock in a saucepan and heat until simmering. In a large heavy saucepan over medium heat, melt the butter. Add the onion and cook until soft and translucent. Add the Arborio rice to the onions and stir for about 3 minutes. Add the wine and stir to prevent sticking as the rice absorbs the wine. Add the stock, 1 cup at a time. The liquid should be absorbed each time, before you add another cup. This should take about 20 minutes—until the rice is cooked tender but with a slight bite in the middle. Add the cheese, olives, and thyme, stirring to combine. Spread mixture on a cookie sheet to cool in the refrigerator. When it has cooled, add the egg and press into small cakes. Fry the cakes in the vegetable oil until lightly golden on both sides. Set aside and keep warm.

### For the Roasted Pepper Coulis

2 red sweet peppers, roasted and chopped
salt and pepper
3 tablespoons extra virgin olive oil, plus more for brushing

½ teaspoon fresh lemon juice
1 teaspoon balsamic vinegar
2 tablespoon fresh basil, chopped
2 tablespoons rinsed capers

PLACE the peppers, salt and pepper, olive oil, lemon juice, vinegar, and fresh basil into a food processor. Pulse until saucy. Add the rinsed capers and set aside.

---

# CORN CAKES

These delicious corn cakes are the ideal accompaniments to grilled meat or fish. They're even nice with eggs for brunch! Use only fresh summer corn.

## Ingredients

1 cup flour
1 tablespoon sugar
½ teaspoon salt
1 teaspoon baking powder
¼ teaspoon smoked paprika
1 cup milk

1 egg
1 teaspoon white vinegar
4 cups corn, cut off the cob
¼ cup green onions, chopped
1 tablespoon vegetable oil for frying

## Preparation

MIX together the flour, sugar, salt, baking powder, and paprika and set aside. In a large mixing bowl whisk together the milk, egg, vinegar, corn and onion. Combine the two mixtures. Heat a large skillet with 1 tablespoon of vegetable oil. When hot, add the batter a scant ¼ cup at a time. Flip when lightly golden. Serve with melted butter.

# CHOCOLATE TOFFEE TART

This tart is one of our customers' favorites. We usually serve it slightly warmed with vanilla bean ice cream.

## Ingredients

1½  cups sugar
½  cup water
1¼  cups heavy cream, warmed
1  egg
1  egg yolk

1  teaspoon vanilla
⅛  teaspoon salt
Tart Crust (recipe follows)
Chocolate Glaze (recipe follows)

## Preparation

PREHEAT oven to 325 degrees. In a medium heavy saucepan, place the sugar and pour the ½ cup water over the top. Making sure the pan is on medium heat, gently swirl the syrup. You want this syrup to clarify before a boil is reached, so keep taking the pan off the heat and swirling mixture until syrup is clear. Once the sugar is completely dissolved, bring mixture to a boil on high heat. Cover pan with a lid and boil furiously for 2 minutes. Uncover the pan and cook the syrup until it turns a nice amber color. Don't burn this! It happens fast.

REMOVE the pan from the heat and pour in the warmed heavy cream. This can splatter, so be careful. Stir until smooth. If the mixture gets lumpy, put the pan over low heat again until it melts. In a medium bowl, whisk together the egg, yolk, vanilla, and salt. Gradually whisk in the toffee mixture.

POUR into the cooled Tart Crust. Bake in 325-degree oven until set, about 45 minutes. Let cool, then glaze with Chocolate Glaze.

*Serves 8*

## For the Tart Crust

2  cups flour
¾  cup powdered sugar
2  teaspoons orange zest

1  egg yolk
14  tablespoons unsalted butter

PREHEAT oven to 350 degrees. Put all ingredients into the food processor until mixture comes together. Pat crust into an 8-inch tart pan. Bake at 350 degrees until lightly golden. Let cool before filling.

## For the Chocolate Glaze

3  ounces bittersweet chocolate

2  tablespoons heavy cream

MELT chocolate in the microwave for 30 seconds. Stir in cream. Spread glaze over the cooled tart.

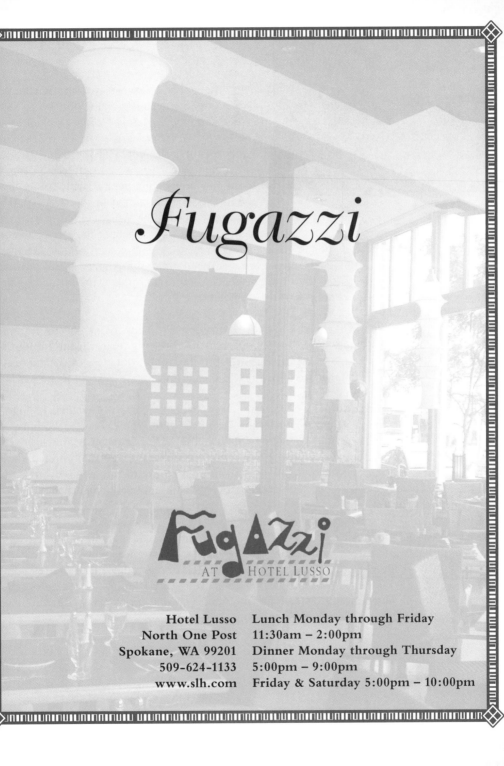

# Fugazzi

Fugazzi

AT HOTEL LUSSO

**Hotel Lusso**
**North One Post**
**Spokane, WA 99201**
**509-624-1133**
**www.slh.com**

**Lunch Monday through Friday**
**11:30am – 2:00pm**
**Dinner Monday through Thursday**
**5:00pm – 9:00pm**
**Friday & Saturday 5:00pm – 10:00pm**

# Fugazzi Restaurant

### *Jason Rex, Executive Chef*

The second largest city in Washington, Spokane was originally founded as "Spokan Falls" in 1872. It draws its name from the Native American tribe known as the Spokane, meaning "Children of the Sun." The falls of the Spokane River were a gathering place for the area's indigenous people, who existed upon the abundance of salmon in the river. With the expansion across the West, the Northern Pacific Railroad was completed to Spokane and brought European settlement to the area. The name of the town was changed to Spokane in 1883, and a bustling commercial center was established. However, in the summer of 1889, a fire destroyed most of this area. In the aftermath of the fire, buildings rose as rapidly as supplies could be brought in. Many of the buildings that were rebuilt were fine examples of the Romanesque Rival style, and still stand proudly in downtown Spokane.

The lush Hotel Lusso, a member of Small Luxury Hotels of the World, occupies one of these beautiful old buildings. Lusso is Italian for luxury, and the extravagantly appointed over-sized guest rooms with 14-foot ceilings attest to the appropriateness of the name. The generous use of marble, detailed scrollwork, and elegant archways carry out the Mediterranean theme of this boutique hotel.

That theme is carried through to the intimate and contemporary Cavallino Lounge as well as the award-winning Fugazzi Restaurant. Occupying the ground floor of the hotel, the restaurant features spacious floor-to-ceiling windows that frame the view of the busy scene at the corner of Post and West Sprague. The contemporary Italian décor in muted shades of gray, stone, and black are complemented by the rust colors of the exposed brick walls and the lofty ceilings are softened with contemporary lighting fixtures constructed of fabric, glass, and wrought iron.

This beautifully chic setting is the perfect backdrop for world-class cuisine. The restaurant serves steaks, seafood, pastas, and vegetarian dishes with specials that take advantage of the seasonal produce and fish available in the area. In 2000, Fugazzi was voted *Restaurant of the Year* by the Hotel/Motel Association, and the Cavallino Lounge, adjacent to the restaurant, was voted *Best Martini Bar in Spokane 2001 – 2002*. Light fare from the Fugazzi Restaurant is available in the lounge. There is also an afternoon wine reception daily from 4:00pm to 6:00pm, with champagne being served on Friday and Saturday.

# FUGAZZI FAMOUS CALAMARI
## *with Cilantro Caper Mayonnaise*

## Ingredients

2 pounds calamari tubes
1 cup graham cracker crumbs
1 cup all-purpose flour
1 tablespoon paprika
1 tablespoon powdered ginger

½ tablespoon cayenne pepper
½ tablespoon red chili flakes
vegetable oil for frying
Cilantro Caper Mayonnaise
(recipe follows)

## Preparation

SLICE calamari into ¼-inch rings, rinse under cold water, and drain well. Mix together the graham cracker crumbs, flour, and spices. Toss the drained calamari rings in this mixture to thoroughly coat.

IN A deep saucepot, bring the vegetable oil to frying temperature. Working in batches, drop the breaded rings into the oil and fry until golden brown. Drain on paper towels, and then serve with the Cilantro Caper Mayonnaise.

### *Serves 4*

## For the Cilantro Caper Mayonnaise

1 cup mayonnaise
½ bunch cilantro, cleaned & stemmed
4 cloves garlic

3 tablespoons capers, drained & rinsed
salt & pepper to taste

PLACE all ingredients in a food processor and blend until smooth. Serve immediately.

# FUGAZZI SIGNATURE SALAD
## with Apple Cider Vinaigrette and Candied Pecans

### Ingredients

Apple Cider Vinaigrette (recipe follows)

organic baby spinach

crumbled Gorgonzola cheese

dried apricots

dried cranberries

Candied Pecans (recipe follows)

### Preparation

TOSS your desired amount of Apple Cider Vinaigrette—a little goes a long way—with organic baby spinach. Place dressed spinach on individual plates and top with cheese, dried fruits, and Candied Pecans. Serve immediately.

### For the Apple Cider Vinaigrette

1 cup apple cider vinegar

1 cup granulated sugar

1 tablespoon dry English mustard

1 tablespoon onion powder

½ teaspoon salt

½ teaspoon freshly ground black pepper

3½ cups canola oil

MIX all ingredients except oil in a blender. With blender on lowest setting, slowly add canola oil until emulsified. Chill for 30 minutes before serving.

### For the Candied Pecans

1 pound pecans

½ cup brown sugar

½ cup granulated sugar

1 teaspoon cinnamon

1 teaspoon nutmeg

1 cup water

PLACE all ingredients in a heavy-bottomed sauté pan and cook on low until sugar crystallizes and looks dry, about 15 minutes.

# FUGAZZI BROCHETTE

## Ingredients

14  ripe Roma tomatoes, small dice
1  small sweet onion, small dice
14  ounces tomato juice
¼  cup Bloody Mary seasoning
¼  cup fresh basil, chopped

1  cup balsamic vinegar
Garlic/Basil Baguettes (recipe follows)
Parmesan cheese and fresh basil, for garnish

## Preparation

IN A bowl, mix together the tomatoes, onion, tomato juice, Bloody Mary seasoning, and chopped basil. Place in refrigerator to chill for 2 hours.

IN A small saucepan, bring balsamic vinegar to a boil and then reduce to a simmer. Cook until vinegar starts to thicken and has reduced by three-quarters. Cool and set aside.

TOAST Garlic/Basil Baguettes under broiler until golden brown. Cut baguettes into serving sizes. To serve, place chilled tomato mixture in a small glass bowl and surround with toasted baguette slices. Drizzle with balsamic reduction and top with fresh Parmesan and basil.

*Serves 4*

## For the Garlic/Basil Baguettes

2  loaves baguette bread
mayonnaise
2  cloves fresh garlic, chopped

8  large leaves fresh basil, chopped
1  cup Parmesan cheese, freshly grated

SPLIT baguette loaves in half lengthwise and spread them with a thin coat of mayonnaise. Sprinkle garlic and then basil on top. Top bread with freshly grated Parmesan, and hold for service.

# BOURBON STILTON SAUCE

This is the ultimate sauce for any steak.

## Ingredients

2 *shallots, thin slice*
2 *cloves fresh garlic, thin slice*
3 *tablespoons unsalted butter*
2 *tablespoons all-purpose flour*

½ *cup bourbon*
4 *cups Veal Stock (recipe follows)*
 *Stilton cheese (can substitute Gorgonzola)*

## Preparation

SAUTÉ shallots and garlic in butter in a sauté pan. Add flour and cook for 3 minutes. Deglaze mixture with bourbon and cook for 1 minute. Add Veal Stock and reduce by half. Take sauce off heat and fold in Stilton cheese.

*Yield: about 2 cups*

## For the Veal Stock

6 *pounds veal bones*
6 *large yellow onions, rough chopped*
2 *heads celery, rough chopped*
10 *carrots, rough chopped*

4 *cups red wine*
8 *cloves fresh garlic*
2 *fresh bay leaves*
2 *gallons water*

PREHEAT oven to 400 degrees. Place veal bones, onions, celery, and carrots in a roasting pan, place in oven and roast until golden brown, about 30 minutes. Immediately after taking roasting pan out of oven, put on medium-high burner and deglaze with red wine, scraping bottom of pan with a wooden spoon. Cook until wine is reduce by half. Add garlic, bay leaves, and water and simmer for 2 hours. Strain stock and discard all solids. Place back on burner and reduce to 4 cups of stock.

# Luna &
# Cafe Marron

*a neighborhood cafe*

*Luna*  *Marron*

| | |
|---|---|
| 5620 S. Perry Street | 144 S. Cannon Street |
| Spokane, WA 99223 | Spokane, WA 99204 |
| 509-448-2383 | 509-456-8660 |
| www.lunaspokane.com | Monday through Friday |
| Monday through Saturday | 7:00am – 10:00pm |
| 11:00am – 10:00pm | Saturday & Sunday |
| Sunday 9:00am – 10:00pm | 8:00am – 10:00pm |

# Luna & Cafe Marron

### *William and Marcia Bond, Proprietors*

William and Marcia Bond have created a culinary domain in Spokane with the award-winning Luna, the neighborhood favorite Cafe Marron, and the wonderful Bouzies Bakery that produces all the breads for both restaurants as well as selling to several other specialty retailers in the Spokane area.

The flagship restaurant, Luna, is perched in a neighborhood high on Spokane's lovely South Hill. It occupies what had been the post office and before that, a greengrocer. The main dining room is a spacious light-filled room with floor-to-ceiling windows and dramatic wrought iron chandeliers hanging from the wood-paneled vaulted ceiling. Softly draped fabrics in earth tones are hung along the walls, adding a rich texture to the room and creating a sense of intimacy for the diners. The marble-topped tables and the rustic country furniture perfectly capture the essence of the room. There is also a delightful rose-enclosed terrace that is covered, lighted, and heated, as well as a magnificent flower garden courtyard for al fresco dining.

The superb wine list at Luna is the product of co-owner and wine buyer, William Bond, who has bought wisely and well over the years. The depth of the list is remarkable. Since William accumulated the cellar over a number of years and often bought vintages before they became popular, there are some true bargains to be found on the list, which has been honored by *Wine Spectator* magazine with its *Award of Excellence*. For those who appreciate superior beers, Luna also has an excellent list of micro brews and imported beers. Rounding out the liquid refreshments is a comprehensive list of fine spirits.

*Cafe Marron (top) and Luna (bottom)*

Just as in the wine list, excellence prevails in the cuisine at Luna. The distinctly Northwest fare features produce, cheese, meat, and fish that has been grown, raised, or line-caught in the region. A wide range of custom apple wood oven pizzas are offered, such as the grilled chicken breast, sweet onion compote, and crisp smoked country bacon, or the potato pizza with wild mushrooms, herbed goat cheese, and balsamic onions. Wild salmon is usually on the menu, such as the Yakutat salmon with leek fennel risotto, winter squash and roasted garlic aioli. Vegetarian entrées are available and are changed daily, based on what is fresh in the market, and succulent meats such as pan seared veal with hand made gnocchi and a merlot-veal stock reduction round out the entrées.

In the summer of 2005, Marcia and William opened another restaurant with a totally different ambiance. Cafe Marron, on a quiet street in Browne's Addition, is housed in a building that was once a garage. Below the four Marron flags are the words, "a neighborhood café," which says it all. This is a friendly, intimate setting where strangers feel comfortable enough to strike up conversations with other diners. The front of the café is whimsically graced with two overhead garage doors that can be opened during pleasant weather to bring the fresh air into the restaurant. Large stands of ornamental grasses grace the area in front of the open doors, creating a gentle buffer to the street side scene. During inclement or cold weather, the doors are lowered without the loss of light, as they are composed of large panes of glass.

The wine list at Cafe Marron, in comparison to Luna, is more limited but is still a very comprehensive list and includes a nice array of wines by the glass. A good selection of beer and spirits is also available.

The food at the cafe continues to bring back neighborhood residents and visitors alike. The breakfast menu offers something for everyone, from French toast made with Bouzies Bakery's challah bread to traditional omelets and quiches as well as a flatiron steak topped with eggs. The lunch scene brings such delights as a salad composed of frisée and escarole with green beans, Dijon vinaigrette, crisp bacon, and topped with a poached egg. Or, you can enjoy an open-faced sandwich with Parmesan crusted eggplant, ricotta cheese, and marinara on toasted bread with Parmesan and basil. The dinner menu sports such mouth

watering fare as hand made squash raviolis with sautéed butternut squash, prosciutto, and finished with a rich cream sauce. Or, try a cinnamon braised chicken over creamy polenta, or blackened halibut served on a bed of penne with black figs, tomatoes, spinach, basil and a lemon cream sauce. Save room for dessert, as the menu is very tempting with such delicacies as the pecan praline bread pudding and the warm maple cake with honey-whipped cream.

The final part of the "Bond trilogy" is the exceptional breads baked at Bousies Bakery. The bakery was named after a small glacial village in the Pyrenees Mountains of France. The clear glacial lake that marks the town was the inspiration behind the bread—pure ingredients and time-honored methods work together to create breads that are as beautiful to look at, as they are delicious to eat. The hand shaped loaves are baked directly on a stone hearth in the specially designed French oven, and are surrounded by steam in the early stages of baking. This process allows the bread to expand generously, before developing its delicious crisp crust. The flour used is grown and milled locally by a collective group of farmers using a sustainable, no-till method of farming.

Award of Excellence - Luna

# Roasted Beet and Squash Salad
## *with Black Currant Vinaigrette and Goat Cheese*

## Ingredients

1 butternut squash
1 large beet
  olive oil
  salt to taste
2 cloves garlic, minced

8 ounces spring mix salad greens
4 ounces goat cheese, crumbled
1–2 ounces Black Currant Vinaigrette
  (recipe follows)

## Preparation

PREHEAT oven to 400 degrees. Peel, seed, and dice the squash into ½-inch cubes. Peel, quarter, and slice the beet into ¼-inch slices. Toss the squash cubes and beet slices in olive oil, salt, and garlic. Roast at 400 degrees for 10–15 minutes, until the edges are golden brown. Remove from oven and allow squash and beets to fully cool. Toss the greens in the Black Current Vinaigrette and garnish with roasted beats, squash, and goat cheese.

*Serves 4*

## For the Black Current Vinaigrette

1 cup black currant vinegar
¼ cup cassis
2 shallots
4 cloves garlic

½ teaspoon pepper
1½ teaspoon salt
2 cups olive oil

COMBINE all ingredients in a blender and blend until smooth.

# Pumpkin Squash Bisque
## *with Fresh Alaskan Snow Crab*

## Ingredients

6 carrots, peeled & rough chopped
4 onions, peeled & rough chopped
2 cloves garlic, peeled & cracked
1 cup olive oil
1⅓ gallons chicken stock
1 butternut squash, peeled, seeded &diced
3 pounds canned pumpkin

2 tablespoons salt
½ cup brown sugar
1 tablespoon ground ginger
1 tablespoon mace
1 pinch cayenne pepper
4 cups heavy cream
2 pounds Alaskan snow crab

## Preparation

IN A large stockpot sweat the carrots, onions, and garlic in the olive oil until the onions are translucent. Add the chicken stock, butternut squash, and canned pumpkin and bring to a boil. Reduce to a simmer and simmer for 45 minutes, or until the squash is soft. Add the salt, sugar and spices.

IN small batches, transfer to a blender and blend until smooth. Return purée to heat and finish with heavy cream. Place 1 to 2 ounces of crab into serving bowls and ladle hot soup over. Serve immediately.

### *Yield: about 4 quarts*

# CIABATTA

This dough is very wet and will require the use of a stand mixer. Note the two-step process. The Poolish is made the night before you make the Ciabatta.

## Ingredients

Poolish (recipe follows)
1 cup flour
¾ cup water

¼ teaspoon instant yeast
1 teaspoon salt
flour for dusting

## Preparation

COMBINE Poolish with flour, water, and yeast in the bowl of your mixer. Using paddle attachment, mix until flour is just incorporated. Add salt and continue to mix on medium speed until dough is fully mixed, approximately 7 minutes. For best results, scrape down sides of bowl periodically as dough mixes to ensure no flour remains in bottom of bowl. When dough is fairly smooth and elastic, scrape into a well-oiled bowl, cover and keep in a warm place until almost double in size, about 2-3 hours.

PREHEAT oven to 500 degrees at least 1 hour before bread is to be baked. After dough has risen, turn onto a generously floured counter and divide in half using a pastry cutter or kitchen knife. Gently transfer loaves to baking sheet and dust tops with flour. Cover with a cotton towel (not terry cloth) and let rise 1 hour.

PLACE breads in oven and mist liberally with water. Close oven, wait 3 minutes and spray with water again. Bake loaves until golden and sound hollow when tapped on the bottom, 25-30 minutes.

### Yield: 2 loaves

## For the Poolish

½ cup flour
½ cup water

1 small pinch instant yeast

THE night before you intend to bake, stir together ingredients until incorporated. Some lumps will still be present. Cover and let stand at room temperature overnight.

# PAN SEARED HALIBUT

### with Lox-wrapped Scallop Served on Horseradish Mash

## Ingredients

2 4-ounce halibut fillets
salt & pepper
paprika
2 scallops
1 small package of lox
2 tablespoons shallots, minced
olive oil

6 ounces white wine
1 ounce lemon juice
1 ounce orange juice
cold butter chips
Horseradish Mash (recipe follows)
minced shallots, for garnish
shrimp oil, for garnish

## Preparation

SEASON fish with salt, pepper, and paprika and keep cool until ready to cook. Wrap scallops with thin strips of lox and season with salt and pepper.

PREHEAT oven to 350 degrees. In a saucepan, caramelize shallots in a little olive oil. Deglaze pan with white wine and add lemon and orange juices. Reduce by half and remove from heat. Whisk in butter until sauce is slightly thick. Keep warm for service.

IN A separate pan, sear halibut and scallops in a little olive oil and finish in oven.

TO SERVE, in a dinner bowl, place a portion of Horseradish Mash. On top of potatoes place your fillet and stack your scallop on top. Drizzle caramelized shallot sauce around plate and garnish with minced shallots and shrimp oil.

### Serves 2

## For the Horseradish Mash

1 head garlic
olive oil
½ pound red potatoes, scrubbed
salt & pepper

½ cup sour cream
horseradish to taste
3 tablespoons chives, chopped

PREHEAT oven to 375 degrees. Cut off bottom of garlic head and place in ovenproof pan. Drizzle olive oil over garlic and roast in oven until tender, about 50 minutes. Let garlic head cool, and then squeeze cloves out. Place potatoes in a pan, cover with water, and simmer until tender. Drain and mash potatoes, adding roasted garlic, salt, pepper, sour cream, horseradish, and chives.

# CHALLAH

## Ingredients

| | |
|---|---|
| 3 cups flour | ½ cup sugar |
| 1½ cups water | ½ cup butter, room temperature |
| 2 eggs | 2 teaspoons salt |
| 1 tablespoon yeast | 1 egg, beaten |
| ⅓ cup milk | 1 tablespoon water |

## Preparation

IN A standup mixer, combine first six ingredients (flour through sugar) until flour is just incorporated. Break butter into small chunks and add along with salt. Mix until dough is smooth and elastic, approximately 7 minutes. Turn into well-oiled bowl, cover, and let stand 2 hours.

DIVIDE dough into 6 equal pieces. Roll each piece into a rope. Using three ropes, braid into a loaf. Place braided loaf on oiled cookie sheet. Combine beaten egg and tablespoon of water and brush the top and sides of each loaf thoroughly. Cover loosely and let stand approximately 1 hour.

PREHEAT oven to 400 degrees. Bake breads in center of oven 35–40 minutes, until loaves are golden and sound hollow when tapped on the bottom.

*Yield: 2 loaves*

# PECAN PRALINE BREAD PUDDING

This recipe is one of my latest creations and has been a big hit on our fall dessert menu, although I think it would be great any time of year. I always keep a bread pudding on the seasonal changing menu because we have great bread from our bakery to use. The hardest part is keeping our staff from snacking on the pralines! — Kaycee Blaylock, Pastry Chef

## Ingredients

5 eggs
1¼ cups whipping cream
1¼ cups milk
¾ cup brown sugar
3 tablespoons maple syrup
2 teaspoons vanilla

5 cups bread, cubed & toasted
1 cup Pecan Pralines, chopped
   (recipe follows)
caramel sauce
vanilla ice cream
chopped pecans, for garnish

## Preparation

PREHEAT oven to 375 degrees. Mix the eggs, cream, milk, sugar, syrup, and vanilla. Pour this mixture over toasted bread cubes. Let sit for at least half an hour or until bread gets soft. Fold in chopped Pecan Pralines.

DIVIDE this mixture into 6 greased ramekins or oven-safe dishes. Bake in water bath in 375-degree oven for approximately 1 hour. They are done when no custard oozes out when pressed. Let sit on counter for 30 minutes and then chill.

SERVE warm with caramel sauce, vanilla ice cream, and more chopped pralines.

*Serves 6*

## For the Pecan Pralines

1 cup pecans
½ cup brown sugar

2 tablespoons heavy cream

PREHEAT oven to 350 degrees. Mix all ingredients together and pour onto a sheet pan lined with parchment. Bake at 350 degrees for 20 minutes.

*A young woman hop picker loosens the heavy twine that holds the hop vines in place on a stake. She wears a loose fitting blouse, long skirt, heavy gloves and a hat. She works at an unidentified hop. September, 1906*

# Riverview Thai

1003 East Trent
Spokane, WA 99202
509-325-8370
www.riverviewthai.com

Lunch Monday through Friday
11:30am – 2:00pm
Dinner Seven Nights
5:00pm – 9:00pm

# Riverview Thai Restaurant

### Bang-Orn, Chef/Owner
### Carl Wilson, Owner

Authentic Thai cooking is among the world's most delicious cuisines, with a unique blend of sweet, piquant, and spicy often highlighted with the citrus flavorings of lemongrass or lime. The use of Asian sauces and coconut milk is also prevalent in many of the dishes.

The city of Spokane is blessed with a family owned and operated restaurant featuring genuine Thai cuisine, prepared by a former resident of Bangkok. Bang-Orn and her husband, Carl Wilson, welcome you to the restaurant along with Chris, Anna, and Mailee. Bang-Orn—her friends and family call her "On"—is the heart and soul of Riverview Thai. Many of the recipes used at the restaurant were passed down family-tradition style and brought over from Thailand by "On." She received her culinary training in Thailand and honed her craft while working in the homes of Bangkok's elite. She is considered a food artist, with her abilities to serve even the most common Thai dishes with a special zest and flavor unequaled outside of Bangkok.

Riverview Thai originally opened in 1991 in the historic 1895 building known as the Spokane Flour Mill. In 2002, the restaurant moved to its new location in the River Walk Mall. The location is larger than the old venue and offers splendid views of the Spokane River from almost any seat in the restaurant. In the summer, outdoor seating is available by the river with umbrella tables, where guests can enjoy the gentle breezes and listen to the flow of the river as it passes the tree-lined banks. Inside, the casual setting features a décor reminiscent of Bangkok with comfortable tables as well as booths. The restaurant also has an elegant banquet room available for parties up to 70. The lofty ceiling sports graceful chandeliers and the huge windows are draped with soft gauzy material that does not interfere with the river scene.

The very extensive menu offers something for everyone's taste. Along with the usual mixture of appetizers, salads, soups, and entrees of beef, pork, poultry, and seafood, the menu also lists curries, noodles, and Thai fried rice selections, as well as special Thai desserts. Of special mention is their unique "Crying Tiger" steak, another Thai marvel based on the "butter knife tender" and juicy, world famous, "Kobe" beef.  The personable wait staff is very knowledgeable about the food and happy to share their thoughts on the various dishes. The restaurant is also very accommodating to the different levels spicy hot seasoning enjoyed by their guests. A wide selection of beers includes micro brews and imported beers, many from Asia, and a nice wine list features wines mainly from Washington and California.

# TOM KHA GAI
## (Chicken & Coconut Milk Soup)

This is a smooth chicken soup that can be as spicy as you want it. It can also be made with shrimp, pork, beef, mushrooms, or tofu. Most of the ingredients can be found in any local oriental market. For the fish sauce, I prefer Thailand brands Tiparos or Ruang Tong. For the coconut milk, I like Chakoah or Arroy Dee brands. — Bang-Orn

## Ingredients

- 2 kaffir lime leaves, fresh or dry
- 16 fluid ounces chicken stock or water
- 1 2-inch piece of lemon grass, slightly crushed to release flavor, or you may cut it into strips
- 1 1-inch cube of galangal ("kha"), thinly sliced
- 4 tablespoons fish sauce, more or less to taste - this provides the "salty"
- 2 tablespoons lime juice, more or less to taste

- 1 4-ounce boneless, skinless, chicken breast cut into bite-sized pieces
- 5 fluid ounces coconut milk or coconut cream - NOT coconut water
  small red chilies, slightly crushed, or Thai chili powder (see note below)
  green onions and cilantro leaves, for garnish

## Preparation

SLICE the kaffir leaves if using fresh leaves. If using dry ones, they should be cracked but not powdered, to release the flavor.

HEAT the stock, add the lime leaves, lemon grass, galangal, fish sauce, and lime juice. Stir thoroughly, bring to a boil, add the chicken, coconut milk, and chilies and bring back to a boil. Lower the heat to keep it simmering and cook for about 2 minutes, until the chicken is cooked through.

SERVE with steamed, white (jasmine) rice or, as the beginning of a full Thai meal.

### Serves 4 with other food, but probably only enough for 2 if eaten as an entrée.

NOTE: You choose how many small red chilies—As hot as you like it but not overdone.

HINT: 2 to 4 small chilies or ¼ to 1 teaspoon of finely ground Thai chili powder is a good start.

# GARLIC SHRIMP

## Ingredients

5 tablespoons garlic, minced
½ ounce vegetable oil
1 ounce oyster sauce
2 ounces Golden Mountain Seasoning
   sauce
2 ounces black soy sauce
1 ounce white cooking wine
¾ cup water

1 tablespoon fish sauce
1 tablespoon sugar
1 teaspoon black pepper
48 shrimp (size 31/40, about 1¼
   pounds) peeled and deveined, tail off
   or tail on, as you desire
   chopped green onions and cilantro, for
   garnish

## Preparation

HEAT wok to medium-high. Fry garlic in oil. Add all ingredients except for shrimp. When sauce begins to boil, add shrimp and stir-fry until shrimp are cooked, about 2½ minutes. Garnish with a sprinkle of chopped green onions and cilantro.

SERVE with hot, steamed "jasmine" rice.

*Serves 6*

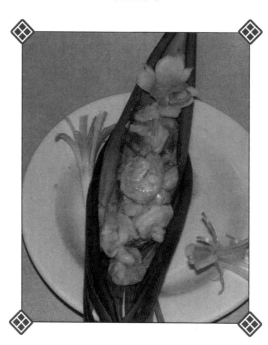

# Ginger Chicken

## Ingredients

1 tablespoon garlic, minced
½ cup fresh ginger, sliced
½ ounce vegetable oil
3 chicken breasts, sliced thin (about 1½ pounds)
¾ cup water
1½ ounces black soy sauce
1 ounce oyster sauce

1 ounce Golden Mountain Seasoning sauce
1 ounce cooking wine
1 tablespoon fish sauce
1 tablespoon sugar
2 green bell peppers, sliced
2 yellow onions, sliced
⅔ cup mushrooms, sliced

## Preparation

HEAT wok to medium-high. Fry garlic and ginger in oil. Add the chicken breasts and ¾ cup water. After chicken is cooked, add all other ingredients, continuously stirring until the vegetables are done.

SERVE with hot, steamed "jasmine" rice.

*Serves 6–8*

# BLACK RICE PUDDING

The Rice Pudding should be served hot. For a delicious variation, try adding a scoop of vanilla or coconut-flavored ice cream with a scoop of rice pudding and drizzle the topping over the entire dessert. Besides the additional flavors, you will enjoy the experience of "hot vs. cold" that accompanies each bite.

## Ingredients

1 cup black rice (raw, uncooked)
Note: This is NOT wild rice!
6 cups water
½ cup sugar

8 ounces (225g) canned coconut milk
(Chakoh brand preferred)
Topping (recipe follows)

## Preparation

RINSE and drain the rice 2 or 3 times. Add the 6 cups of water and bring it to a boil. Reduce the heat to a slow simmer; cover, and cook for 45 minutes or until soft. Add the sugar and coconut milk. Stir well and cook for 10 more minutes. There should be no standing water after the cooking, it should all be absorbed into the rice and sugar mix.

TO SERVE, place portions of the rice pudding in bowls, and pour a small amount topping over the rice pudding.

*Serves 4*

## For the Topping

½ cup coconut milk
½ teaspoon salt

2 tablespoons sugar

COMBINE and mix the topping ingredients and hold for service.

*For many years the San Juan Islands have been a favorite place for camping. This photo, taken in the San Juans, shows a large group of campers relaxing in the grass outside a tent by the shore. One woman uses an umbrella to shade herself from the sun. A boy lies on his stomach and reads a book. Judging by the clothing, the photo was probably taken sometime between 1902 and 1910.*

# GLOSSARY

| | |
|---|---|
| *aioli* | A mayonaise base, strongly seasoned with garlic or other seasoning. |
| *baste* | To spoon liquid over food as it cooks, usually fat or drippings, which keeps the food moist. |
| *beurre blanc* | A sauce composed of wine, vinegar, shallots, and butter; literally "white butter" in French. |
| *blanch* | To plunge food (usually vegetables or fruits) into boiling water briefly, then into cold water to stop the cooking process. |
| *braise* | To brown food (usually meats or vegetables) first in fat, then cook, covered, in a small amount of liquid at low heat for a long time. |
| *brioche* | A French pastry bread made rich with butter and eggs that is used not only for desserts, but also in many meat and cheese dishes. |
| *brodetto* | The Italian version of Bouillabaisse, it is a soup containing a variety of fish and shellfish. Its origin dates much earlier than the French version. |
| *brunoise* | A mixture of vegetables that have been finely diced or shredded, then cooked slowly in butter. |
| *canela* | The Spanish word for cinnamon, it usually refers to the softer loose-bark variety rather than hard-stick cinnamon. |
| *caul* | A fatty membrane from the stomach of pigs or sheep. It is often used to wrap pâtés. |
| *chiffonade* | Similar to julienne, the process of cutting lettuce, endive, or herbs into thin even strips. |
| *chinois* | A very fine mesh cone-shaped metal sieve used for puréeing or straining. Often a spoon or pestle is used to press the food through it. |
| *cioppino* | This fish stew, usually with a tomato base, includes a variety of fish and shellfish. |
| *crème fraîche* | A thick, velvety cream that is slightly tangy and can be boiled without curdling. Can be purchased in gourmet markets, or made at home by adding buttermilk to heavy cream. |
| *de-beard* | To pull the threads towards the hinge of the mussel and tear out. |
| *deglaze* | To add liquid, usually wine or stock, to the skillet to loosen browned bits of food left from sauteing or browning. |
| *demi-glace* | A rich brown sauce (usually meat stock) combined with Madeira or sherry and slowly cooked until it's reduced by at least half, to a thick glaze. |
| *diver scallops* | Scallops that are actually collected by hand by divers, instead of being netted by boat. This is a more eco-friendly way of harvesting scallops. They are often less gritty than those dragged by a net. |
| *emulsify* | To blend together 2 or more liquids that do not naturally blend, such as oil and vinegar. Done by whisking the ingredients together with an emulsifier such as an egg yolk or milk. |
| *fond* | A French term for stock. |

| | |
|---|---|
| *galanga;* *galangal;* *galingale* | Part of the ginger family, this root is used in the foods of Thailand, Laos, and Cambodia. It is very pungent & has a fiery flavor. |
| *gastrique* | A mixture of vinegar and sugar that is reduced until almost evaporated. Usually used in sauces made with fruit. |
| *gremolata* | A garnish added to a cooked dish, such as osso buco, for a fresh accent. It usually consists of minced parsley, citrus zest, garlic, oil, and salt. |
| *Kaffir lime leaf* | Essential in many Thai soups and curries, it has an unmistakable and refreshing taste and aroma that can not really be substituted. The leaves are double and dark glossy green. |
| *ketjap manis;* *kecap manis* | A rich, dark, syrupy sauce, similar to soy sauce, but sweeter. Often used in marinades and as a flavoring in Indonesian dishes, it can be found in Asian markets. |
| *lardons;* *lardoons* | A French term for narrow strips of fat used to lard meats, sometimes used for bacon that has been diced, blanched, and fried. |
| *malpoora* | A term in Indian cooking for sweet whole wheat cakes |
| *mascarpone* | An Italian cream cheese, double- to triple-rich and buttery. |
| *mirepoix;* *mirepois* | A mixture of diced carrots, onion, celery, and herbs that is sautéed in butter. |
| *mirin; aji mirin* | A sweet, rice wine used in cooking to sweeten meat or fish dishes. |
| *nappe* | A term indicating the thickness of a liquid, usually described as thick enough to coat the back of a spoon. |
| *panna cotta* | Literally means "cooked cream" in Italian. A light, silky egg custard, often flavored with caramel. Served cold, usually with fruit or chocolate sauce. |
| *penne lisce* | Lisce is the Italian adjective for smooth. This penne has smooth walls, instead of the ridged walls of penne rigate. |
| *Plugrá* | A brand of European butter that is richer in fat and has less water content than regular butter. It works especially well when making pastries. |
| *pluot* | A hybrid fruit developed in the 20th century, it is a cross between a plum and an apricot. It is a very sweet, smooth-skinned fruit. |
| *preserved lemon* | Popular ingredient in Moroccan cuisine. Lemons are preserved in a mix of lemon juice and salt for up to 30 days. Other spices are sometimes added. |
| *rouille* | A paste of hot chiles, garlic, olive oil, bread crumbs, and stock. Saffron is sometimes added. Used in bouillabaisse and other fish stews. |
| *roux* | A mixture of equal parts flour and butter used to thicken sauces. Cooking different lengths of time results in different flavors and colors. |
| *sec* | French word for "dry". |
| *slurry* | A thin mixture of water and flour or cornstarch used as a thickener. |
| *verjus* | A French word for "green juice," it is the unfermented juice of semi-ripe grapes, usually harvested during the crop-thinning of wine grapes. High in acid and low in sugar, the juice is tart, but not tart like vinegar. |

# Culinary Sources

This list is provided for your convenience. While many of the suggested suppliers have been recommended, not all suppliers have been individually checked out. We do not endorse any particular vendor or supplier.

**Broken Arrow Ranch**
Antelope, venison, wild boar, sausages
Ingram, TX
800-962-4263
www.brokenarrowranch.com

**Caviar Direct**
Foreign & domestic caviar
800-650-2828
www.caviar-direct.com

**Chef Depot**
Everything for the chef, including cutlery, cookware, and gourmet food
630-739-5200
www.chefdepot.com

**Ethnic Grocer**
Authentic foods from all over the world
Bensenville, IL
312-373-1777
www.ethnicgrocer.com

**Fungi Perfecti, LLC**
Truffles, truffle oils, truffle purées, as well as comprehensive info on mushroom, including mushroom growing products
Olympia, WA
800-780-9126
www.fungi.com

**Gourmet Foodstore**
Foie gras, pâté, caviar, truffles, and other gourmet products
www.gourmetfoodstore.com

**Nash Huber's Organic Produce**
1865 East Anderson Road
Sequim, WA 98382
360-683-4642
www.nashsproduce.com

**Just Smoked Salmon**
Cedar and alder cooking planks, as well as fresh and smoked seafood, including smoked oysters and clams
866-716-2710
www.justsmokedsalmon.com

**Local Harvest**
Locate food sources by state
www.localharvest.org

**Oakwood Game Farms**
Fresh & smoked gamebirds, wild rice
Princeton, MN
800-328-6647
www.oakwoodgamefarm.com

**Pacific Northwest Shop**
Gourmet mustards, dips, and rubs from the Pacific Northwest
2702 N. Proctor Street
Tacoma, WA 98407
800-942-3523
www.pacificnorthwestshop.com

**Penzey's Spices**
Spices, herbs, and seasonings
800-741-7787

**Prairie Harvest Specialty Foods**
Game meat, mushrooms, berries, foie gras
Spearfish, SD
800-350-7166
www.prairieharvest.com

**Sea Bear**
Cedar grilling planks, smoked salmon, fresh seafood, as well as chowders, bisques, sauces, and rubs.
605 30th Street
Anacortes, WA 98221
800-645-3474
www.seabear.com

**Seattle Gourmet Foods**
Gourmet foods of the Pacific Northwest
19016 72nd Avenue
Kent, WA 98032
800-800-9490 – Ext 100
www.seattlegourmetfoods.com

**Made in Washington**
Washington food products, wines, and cookbooks
Shop online or locate stores in and around Seattle.
800-338-9903
www.madeinwashington.com

**Snake River Farms**
Kobe beef and Kurobuta pork
Boise, ID
www.snakeriverfarms.com

**Terra Sonoma Food Company**
For verjus
P.O. Box 444
Geyserville, CA 95441
707-431-1382
www.terrasonoma.com

**Temple of Thai**
Online store for Thai foods
www.templeofthai.com

**Valley Game & Gourmet**
Game meats, foie gras, patés plus recipes
Wholesale site: www.valleygame.com
Retail site: www.dinewild.com

# Photo Copyrights/Credits

**Front Cover, left to right:** ©Brix 25°; ©McMillan's; ©Christopher's; ©The Inn at Langley; ©Timothy J Park (for The Depot); ©Seattle Museum of History and Industry; ©Seattle Museum of History and Industry; ©Brix 25°; ©Salish Lodge; ©Brix 25°; ©Washington State Historical Society, Tacoma - Curtis - 44745; ©Wild Coho;
**Back Cover, left to right:** ©Stars at Semiahoo Resort; ©Wild Coho; ©Lake Cresent Lodge; ©Duck Soup Inn; ©Port Ludlow Resort; ©Salish Lodge;

**all interior photos:** ©Tracy Johnson or as noted below

**i:** ©Snoqualmie Valley Historical Museum; **viii(big):** ©Snoqualmie Valley Historical Museum; **viii(small):** ©Seattle Museum of History and Industry; **xii (top):** ©Washington State Historical Society, Tacoma - 2006.0.269; **xii(bottom):** ©Snoqualmie Valley Historical Museum; **1,2,4:** ©Stars at Semiahoo Resort; **7,8,10,14:** ©McMIllan's; **15,16,21:** ©Duck Soup Inn; **27,28:** ©Il Posto; **34:** ©Christopher's; **39,40,43:** ©The Inn at Langley; **46,48:** ©Port Ludlow Resort; **50:** ©Snoqualmie Valley Historical Museum; **55:** ©The Wild Coho; **65,66,71:** ©Toga's; **74,79,81:** ©Lake Cresent Lodge; **82:** ©Seattle Museum of History and Industry; **84,87:** ©Ocean Crest Resort; **90,93:** ©The Depot; **96:** ©Seattle Museum of History and Industry; **101:** ©Washington State Historical Society, Tacoma - Curtis - 7581; **106:** ©Seattle Museum of History and Industry; **108,113,115,117:** ©Brix 25°; **118:** ©Seattle Museum of History and Industry; **120,123:** ©Salish Lodge; **128,129,130:** ©Inna's Cuisine; **134:** ©Seattle Museum of History and Industry; **142:** ©Washington State Historical Society, Tacoma - Curtis - 44745; **144,145:** ©Tendril's; **150:** ©Greystone; **155,156,159,161,163(top),165:** ©Taverna Tagaris: **168,170,171:** ©Whitehouse-Crawford; **174:** ©Seattle Museum of History and Industry; **176,181:** ©Whoopemup Hollow Café; **182:** ©Seattle Museum of History and Industry; **184:** ©Weinhard Café; **197:** ©Luna & Cafe Marron; **204:** ©Washington State Historical Society, Tacoma - Curtis - 7584; **206,208:** ©Riverview Thai; **211:** ©Seattle Museum of History and Industry;

# ABOUT THE PUBLISHERS

Chuck and Blanche started Wilderness Adventures Press, Inc. in 1993, publishing outdoor and sporting books. Along with hunting and fishing, they love fine dining, good wines, and traveling. They have always been able to "sniff out" the most outstanding and interesting restaurants in any city they visit.

On weekends, they experiment in the kitchen, cooking a variety of fish and meats, as well as preparing the harvest from their time in the field. This love of cooking has resulted in a large library of cookbooks, and has inspired them to create a series of cookbooks based on their love of travel and fine dining.

Chuck and Blanche make their home in Gallatin Gateway, Montana, along with their four German wirehaired pointers.

# INDEX

# NOTES

# NOTES

# NOTES

# NOTES